A Domestic Problem

Work and Culture in the Household

Abby Morton Diaz

Contents

CHAPTER I.   TAKING A VIEW OF THE SITUATION. 7

CHAPTER II.   ONE CAUSE OF THE SITUATION.--A PART OF
               "WOMAN'S MISSION" CONSIDERED. 13

CHAPTER III.   CULTURE PROVED TO BE A NEED OF THE
               CHILD-TRAINER. 18

CHAPTER IV.   THE OTHER PART OF "WOMAN'S MISSION."
               --RUFFLES VERSUS READING.--THE CULTIVATION OF
               THE FINGERS. 22

CHAPTER V.   OTHER CAUSES CONSIDERED.--MASCULINE
               IDEA OF WOMAN'S WORK. 26

CHAPTER VI.   REASONS FOR A CHANGE.--THE EARLY
               TRAINING OP WOMEN.--COMMON FALLACIES.--
               THE EDUCATION OF MOTHERS. 31

CHAPTER VII.   A WAY OUT. 34

CHAPTER VIII. SUGGESTIONS FOR LECTURE TOPICS. 40

CHAPTER IX.   WAYS OF IMMEDIATE ESCAPE. 46

CHAPTER X.   MEANS OF ESCAPE ALREADY IN OPERATION. 56

CHAPTER XI.   SUPPLEMENTARY. 62

A DOMESTIC PROBLEM

WORK AND CULTURE IN THE HOUSEHOLD

BY

Abby Morton Diaz

CHAPTER I.
TAKING A VIEW OF THE SITUATION.

Our problem is this: How may woman enjoy the delights of culture, and at the same time fulfil her duties to family and household? Perhaps it is not assuming too much to say, that, in making known the existence of such a problem, we have already taken the first step toward its solution, just as a ship's crew in distress take the first step toward relief by making a signal which calls attention to their needs.

The next step--after having, as we may say, set our flag at half-mast--is one which, if all we hear be true, should come easily to women in council, namely, talking. And talking we must have, even if, as in the social game called "Throwing Light," much of it is done at a venture. In that interesting little game, after a few hints have been given concerning "the word," different members of the company begin at once to talk about it, and think about it, and suggest and hazard descriptive remarks, according to the idea each has formed of it; that is, they try, though in the dark, to "throw light." As the interest increases, the excitement becomes intense. Many of the ideas expressed are absurdly wide of the mark, yet even these help to show what the answer is not; and often, by their coming in contact, a light is struck which helps amazingly. And so, in regard to our problem, we have the hints; then why not begin at once to think about it, and talk about it, and suggest, and guess, and throw light with all our might? No matter if we even get excited, say absurd things, say utterly preposterous things, make blunders. Blunders are to be expected. Let them fly right and left; by hitting together right smartly they may strike out sparks which shall help us find our way.

We all have heard of the frank country girl who said to her bashful lover, "Do say something, if it isn't quite so bright!" This, doubtless, is what every thoughtful woman, if she expressed the sincere desire of her heart regarding our perplexing question, would say to all other women; and it is to comply with that wish, partly expressed to me, that I have gathered up from chance observation, chance reading, and hearsay, some ideas bearing on the subject. Suppose we begin by looking about us, and making clear to our minds just what this state of things is, which, because it hinders culture, many deem so unsatisfactory. After that, we will consider its causes, reasons for changing it, and the way or ways out of it.

A few, a very few, of our women are able to live and move and have their being literally regardless of expense. These can buy of skilled assistants and competent supervisors, whole lifetimes of leisure; with these, therefore, our problem has no concern. The larger class, the immense majority, either do their work themselves, or attend personally to its being done by others; "others" signifying that inefficient, untrustworthy, unstable horde who come fresh from their training in peat-bog and meadow, to cook our dinners, take care of our china dishes, and adjust the nice little internal arrangements of our dwellings.

Observing closely the lives of the immense majority, I think we shall see, that, in conducting their household affairs, the object they have in view is one and the same. I think we shall see that they all strive, some by their own labors wholly, the rest by covering over and piecing out the shortcomings of "help," to present a smooth, agreeable surface to husbands and company. This smooth, agreeable surface may be compared to a piece of mosaic work composed of many parts. Of the almost infinite number of those parts, and of the time, skill, and labor required to adjust them, it hath not entered, it cannot enter, into the heart of man to conceive.

I wonder how long it would take to name, just merely to name, all the duties which fall upon the woman who, to use a common phrase, and a true one, carries on the family. Suppose we try to count them, one by one. Doing this will help to give us that clear view of the present state of things which it is our present object to obtain; though the idea reminds me of what the children used to say when I was a child, "If you count the stars you'll drop down dead,"--a saying founded, probably, on the vastness of the undertaking compared with human endurance. It certainly cannot be called trivial to enumerate the duties to which woman consecrates so large a portion of her life, especially when we remember that into each and all of these duties she has to carry her mind. Where woman's mind must go, woman's mind or man's mind, should not scorn to follow. So let us make the attempt; and we need not stand upon the order of our counting, but begin anywhere.

Setting tables; clearing them off; keeping lamps or gas-fixtures in order; polishing stoves, knives, silverware, tinware, faucets, knobs, &c.; washing and wiping dishes; taking care of food left at meals; sweeping, including the grand Friday sweep, the limited daily sweep, and the oft-recurring dustpan sweep; cleaning paint; washing looking-glasses, windows, window-curtains; canning and preserving fruit; making sauces and jellies, and "catchups" and pickles; making and baking bread, cake, pies, puddings; cooking meats and vegetables; keeping in nice order beds, bedding, and bedchambers; arranging furniture, dusting, and "picking up;" setting forth, at their due times and in due order, the three meals; washing the clothes; ironing, including doing up shirts and other "starched things;" taking care of the baby, night and day; washing and dressing children, and regulating their behavior, and making or getting made, their clothing, and seeing that the same is in good repair, in good taste, spotless from dirt, and suited both to the weather and the occasion; doing for herself what her own personal needs require; arranging flowers; entertaining company; nursing the sick; "letting down" and "letting out" to suit the growing ones; patching, darning, knitting, crocheting, braiding, quilting,--but let us remember the warning of the old saying, and forbear in time.

This, however, is only a general enumeration. This is counting the stars by constellations. Examining closely these items: we shall find them made up each of a number of smaller items, and each of these again of items still smaller. What seem homogeneous are heterogeneous; what seem simple are complex. Make a loaf of bread. That has a simple sound, yet the process is complex. First, hops, potatoes, flour, sugar, water, salt, in right proportions for the yeast. The yeast for raising the yeast must be in just the right condition, and added when the mixture is of just the right temperature. In "mixing up" bread, the temperature of the atmosphere must be considered, the temperature of the water, the situation of the dough. The dough must rise quickly, must rise just enough and no more, must be baked in an oven just hot enough and no hotter, and must be "tended" while baking.

Try clearing off tables. Remove food from platters, care for the remnants, see that nothing is wasted, scrape well every plate, arrange in piles, carry out, wash in soap and water, rinse in clear water, polish with dry cloth, set away in their places,--three times a day.

Taking care of the baby frequently implies carrying the child on one arm while working with the other, and this often after nights made sleepless by its "worrying." "I've done many a baking with a child on my hip," said a farmer's wife in my hearing.

But try now the humblest of household duties, one that passes for just nothing at all; try dusting. "Take a cloth, and brush the dust off,"--stated in this general way, how easy a process it seems! The particular interpretation, is that you move, wipe, and replace every article in the room, from the piano down to the tiniest ornament; that you "take a cloth," and go over every inch of accessible surface, including panelling, mop-boards, window frames and sashes, looking-glass-frames, picture-frames and cords, gas or lamp fixtures; reaching up, tiptoeing, climbing, stooping, kneeling, taking care that not even in the remotest corner shall appear one inch of undusted surface which any slippered individual, leaning back in his arm-chair, can spy out.

These are only a few examples; but a little observation and an exceedingly little experience will show the curious inquirer that there is scarcely one of the apparently simple household operations which cannot be resolved and re-resolved into minute component parts. Thus dusting, which seems at first to consist of simply a few brushes with a cloth or bunch of feathers, when analyzed once, is found to imply the careful wiping of every article in the room, and of all the woodwork; analyzed again, it implies following the marks of the cabinet-maker's tools in every bit of carving and grooving; analyzed again, introducing a pointed stick under the cloth in turning corners. In fact, the investigator of household duties must do as does a distinguished scientist in analyzing matter,--"continue the process of dividing as long as the parts can be discerned," and then "prolong the vision backward across the boundary of experimental evidence." And, if brave enough to attempt to count them, he must bear in mind that what appear to be blank intervals, or blurred, nebulous spaces, are, in reality, filled in with innumerable little duties which, through the glass of observation, may be discerned quite plainly. Let him also bear in mind, that these household duties must be done over and over, and over and over, and as well, each time, as if done to last forever; and, above all, that they every one require mind.

Many a common saying proves this last point. "Put your mind on your work." "Your mind must be where your work is." "She's a good hand to take hold, but she hasn't any calculation." "She doesn't know how to forecast her work." "She doesn't know how to forelay." "Nancy's gittin' past carryin' her mind inter her work. Wal, I remember when I begun to git past carryin' my mind inter my work," said an old woman of ninety, speaking of her sixty-years-old daughter. The old couplet,

> "Man works from rise till set of sun,
> But woman's work is never done,"--

tells the truth. "Woman's work," as now arranged, is so varied, so all-embracing, that it cannot be "done." For every odd moment some duty lies in wait. And it is generally the case, that these multi-form duties press for performance, crowds of them at once. "So many things to be done right off, that I don't know which to take hold of first." "'Tis just as much as I can do to keep my head above water." "Oh, dear! I can't see through!" "My work drives me." "I never know what 'tis not to feel hurried." "The things I can't get done tire me more than the things I do." Such remarks have a meaning.

And those who keep "a girl" have almost equal difficulty in always presenting the smooth, agreeable surface just now spoken of. With the greater ability to hire help comes usually the desire to live in more expensive houses, and to furnish the same with more costly furniture. Every article added is a care added, and the nicer the article the nicer the care required. More, also, is demanded of these in the way of appearance, style, and social civilities; and the wear and tear of superintending "a girl" should by no means be forgotten. At any rate, the complaint, "no time to read," is frequent among women, and is not confined to any one class.

We see, then, that in the present state of things it is impossible for woman-- that is, the family woman, the house-mother--to enjoy the delights of culture. External activities, especially the two insatiable, all-devouring ones which know neither end nor beginning,--housework and sewing-work,--these demand her time, her energies, in short, demand herself,--the whole of her. Yes, the whole, and more too; there is not enough of her to go round. There might possibly be enough, and even something left to spend on culture, were she in sound physical condition; but, alas! a healthy woman is scarcely to be found. This point, namely, the prevailing invalidism of woman, will come up for consideration by and by, when we inquire into the causes of the present state of things. It is none too early, however, to make a note of what some physicians say in regard to it. "Half of all who are born," says one medical writer, "die under twenty years of age; while four-fifths of all who reach that age, and die before another score, owe their death to causes which were originated in their teens. This is a fact of startling import to fathers and mothers, and shows a fearful responsibility." Another medical writer says, "Beside the loss of so many children (nearly twenty-five per cent), society suffers seriously from those who survive, their health being irremediably injured while they are still infants.... Ignorance and injudicious nursery management lie at the root of this evil."

We must be sure not to forget that this prevailing invalidism of women, which is one hinderance to their obtaining culture, can be traced directly back to the ignorance of mothers, for this point has an important bearing on the solution of our problem.

CHAPTER II.
ONE CAUSE OF THE SITUATION.--A PART OF "WOMAN'S MISSION" CONSIDERED.

The question, How may work and culture be combined? was recently submitted, in my hearing, to a highly intelligent lady. She answered with a sigh, "It can't be done. I've tried it; but, as things are now, it can't be done." By "as things are now" she meant, with the established ideas regarding dress, food, appearance, style, and the objects for which woman should spend her time and herself. Suppose we investigate the causes of the present state of things, which, as being a hinderance to culture, is to us so unsatisfactory. A little reflection will enable us to discover several. Chief among them all, I think, is one which may require close inspection before it is recognized to be such. It seems to me that the great underlying cause--the cause of all the other causes--is the want of insight, the unenlightemnent, which prevails concerning, not what woman's mission is, but the ways and means by which she is to accomplish it. Let us consider this.

Those who claim the right of defining it never can say often enough that the true, mission of woman is to train up her children rightly, and to make home happy; and no doubt we all agree with them. But have we, or have they, a full sense of what woman requires to fit her even for the first of these duties? Suppose a philosopher in disguise on a tour of observation from some distant isle or planet should favor us with a visit. He finds himself, we will say, on a spot not a hundred miles from New York or Boston or Chicago. Among the objects which attract his attention are the little children drawn along in their little chaises.

"Are these beautiful creatures of any value?" he asks of a bystander.

"Certainly. They are the hope of the country. They will grow up into men and women who will take our places."

"I suppose there is no danger of their growing up any other than the right kind of men and women, such as your country needs?"

"On the contrary, there is every danger. Evil influences surround them from their birth. These beautiful creatures have in them the possibilities of becoming mean, base, corrupt, treacherous, deceitful, cruel, false, revengeful; of becoming, in fact, unworthy and repulsive in many ways. Why, all our criminals, our drunkards, liars, thieves, burglars, murderers, were once innocent little children like these!"

"And whether these will become like those, or not, depends on chance?"

"Oh, no! It depends largely on training, especially on early training. Children are like wax to receive impressions, like marble to retain them."

"Are they constituted pretty nearly alike, so that the treatment which is best for one is best for all?"

"By no means. Even those in the same family are often extremely unlike. They have different temperaments, dispositions, propensities. Some require urging, others checking. Some do better with praise, others without; the same of blame. It requires thought and discernment to know what words to speak, how many to speak, and when to speak them. In fact, a child's nature is a piece of delicate, complex machinery, and each one requires a separate study; for, as its springs of action are concealed, the operator is liable at any time to touch the wrong one."

"And mistakes here will affect a child through its whole lifetime?"

"They will affect it through all eternity." "But who among you dare make these early impressions which are to be so enduring? Who are the operators on these delicate and complex pieces of mental machinery?"

"Oh! the mothers always have the care of the children. This is their mission,-- the chief duty of their lives."

"But how judicious, how comprehensive, must be the course of education which will fit a person for such an office!"

"Do you think so? Hem! Well, it is not generally considered that a woman who is going to marry and settle down to family life needs much education."

"You mean, doubtless, that she only receives the special instruction which her vocation requires."

"Special instruction?"

"Yes. If woman's special vocation is the training of children, of course she is educated specially with a view to that vocation."

"Well, I never heard of such a kind of education. But here is one of our young mothers: she can tell you all about it."

We will suppose, now, that our philosopher is left with the young mother, who names over what she learned at the "institute."

"And the training of children--moral, intellectual, and physical--was no doubt made a prominent subject of consideration."

"Training of children? Oh, no! That would have been a curious kind of study."

"Where, then, were you prepared for the duties of your mission?"

"What mission do you mean?"

"Your mission of child-training."

"I had no preparation."

"No preparation? But are you acquainted with the different temperaments a child may have, and the different combinations of them? Are you competent to the direction and culture of the intellectual and moral nature? Have you skill to touch the hidden springs of action? Have you, thus uninstructed, the power, the knowledge, the wisdom, requisite for guiding that mighty force, a child's soul?"

"Alas! there is hardly a day that I do not feel my ignorance on all these points."

"Are there no sources from which knowledge may be obtained? There must be books written on these subjects."

"Possibly; but I have no time to read them."

"No time?--no time to prepare for your chief mission?"

"It is our mission only in print. In real life it plays an extremely subordinate part."

"What, then, in real life, is your mission?"

"Chiefly cooking and sewing."

"Your husband, then, does not share the common belief in regard to woman's chief duty."

"Oh, yes! I have heard him express it many a time; though I don't think he comprehends what a woman needs in order to do her duty by her children. But he loves them dearly. If one should die he would be heart-broken."

"Is it a common thing here for children to die?"

"I am grieved to say that nearly one-fourth die in infancy."

"And those who live,--do they grow up in full health and vigor?"

"Oh, indeed they do not! Why, look at our crowded hospitals! Look at the apothecaries' shops at almost, every corner. Look at the advertisements of medicines. Don't you think there's meaning in these, and a meaning in the long rows of five-story swell-front houses occupied by physicians, and a meaning in the people themselves? There's scarcely one of them but has some ailment."

"But is this matter of health subject to no laws?"

"The phrase, 'laws of health,' is a familiar one, but I don't know what those laws are." "Mothers, then, are not in the habit of teaching them to their children?"

"They are not themselves acquainted with them."

"Perhaps this astonishing ignorance has something to do with the fearful mortality among infants. Do not husbands provide their wives with books and other means of information on this subject?"

"Generally speaking, they do nothing of the kind."

"And does not the subject of hygienic laws, as applied to the rearing of children, come into the courses of study laid out for young women!"

"No, indeed. Oh, how I wish it had!--and those other matters you mentioned. I would give up every thing else I ever learned for the sake of knowing how to bring up my children, and how to keep them in health."

"The presidents and professors of your educational institutions,--do they share the common belief as to woman's mission?"

"Oh, yes! They all say that the chief business of woman is to train up her children."

(*Philosopher's solo*.)

"There seems to be blindness and stupidity somewhere among these people. From what they say of the difficulty of bringing up their children, it must take an archangel to do it rightly; still they do not think a woman who is married and settles down to family life needs much education! Moreover, in educating young women, that which is universally acknowledged to be the chief business of their lives receives not the least attention."

If our philosopher continued his inquiries into the manners and customs of our country, he must have felt greatly encouraged; for he would have found that it is only in this one direction that we show such blindness and stupidity. He would have found that in every other occupation we demand preparation. The individual who builds our ships, cuts our coats, manufactures our watches, superintends our machinery, takes charge of our cattle, our trees, our flowers, must know how, must have been especially prepared for his calling. It is only character-moulding, only shaping the destinies of immortal beings, for which we demand neither preparation nor a knowledge of the business. It is only of our children that we are resigned to lose nearly one-fourth by death, "owing to ignorance and injudicious nursery management." Were this rate of mortality declared to exist among our domestic animals, the community would be aroused at once.

CHAPTER III.
CULTURE PROVED TO BE A NEED OF THE CHILD-TRAINER.

Perhaps some day the community may come to perceive that woman requires for her vocation what the teacher, the preacher, the lawyer, and the physician, require for theirs; namely, special preparation and general culture. The first, because every vocation demands special preparation; and the second, because, to satisfy the requirements of young minds, she will need to draw from almost every kind of knowledge. And we must remember here, that the advantages derived from culture are not wholly an intellectual gain. We get from hooks and other sources of culture not merely what informs the mind, but that which warms the heart, quickens the sympathies, strengthens the understanding; get clearness and breadth of vision, get refining and ennobling influences, get wisdom in its truest and most comprehensive sense; and all of these, the last more than all, a mother needs for her high calling. That it is a high calling, we have high authority to show. Dr. Channing says, "No office can compare in importance with that of training a child." Yet the office is assumed without preparation.

Herbert Spencer asks, in view of this omission, "What is to be expected when one of the most intricate of problems is undertaken by those who have given scarcely a thought as to the principles on which its solution depends? Is the unfolding of a human being so simple a process that any one may superintend and regulate it with no preparation whatever?... Is it not madness to make no provision for such a task?"

Horace Mann speaks out plainly, and straight to the point. "If she is to prepare a refection of cakes, she fails not to examine some cookery-book or some manuscript receipt, lest she should convert her rich ingredients into unpalatable compounds; but without ever having read one book upon the subject of education, without ever having sought one conversation with an intelligent person upon it, she undertakes so to mingle the earthly and celestial elements of instruction for that child's soul that he shall be fitted to discharge all duties below, and to enjoy all blessings above." And again, "Influences imperceptible in childhood, work out more and more broadly into beauty or deformity in after life. No unskilful hand should ever play upon a harp where the tones are left forever in the strings."

In a newspaper I find this amusingly significant sentence: "Truthfully, indeed, do the Papists boast that the Episcopal Church is training-ground for Rome. The female mind is frequently enticed by display of vestments and music; and, if the Ritualists can pervert the mothers, they know that the next generation is theirs." This is significant, because it signifies that, however weak and easy of enticement the "female mind" may be, it has a mighty power to influence the young.

But we can show not only opinions and prophecies, but the results of actual scientific experiments. A recent number of "The Popular Science Monthly" contains an account of experiments made in Jamaica upon the mental capacity for learning of the different races there existing. The experimenter found, he says, "unequal speed," but saw "nothing which can be unmistakably referred to difference of race. The rate of improvement is due almost entirely to the relative elevation of the home circle in which the children live. Those who are restricted to the narrowest gauge of intellectual exercise live in such a material and coarse medium that their mental faculties remain slumbering; while those who hear at home of many things, and are brought up to intellectual employments, show a corresponding proficiency in learning."

This, and the editor's comments, bear directly on our side, that is to say, the culture side. The editor says it is inevitable "that the medium in which the child is habitually immersed, and by which it is continually and unconsciously impressed, should have much greater value in the formation of mental character than the mere lesson experiences of school. Home education is, after all, the great fact; and it is domestic influences by which the characters of children are formed. Where men are exhausted by business, and women are exhausted by society (or other means), we may be pretty sure that but little can be done to shape and conduct the home with a reference to the higher mental needs of the children who live in it."

Now, who, more than any one, "shapes and conducts the home"? Who creates these "domestic influences," this "medium in which the child is habitually immersed"? Woman. In the name of common sense, then, throw open to woman every avenue of knowledge. Surround her with all that will elevate and refine. Give her the highest, broadest, truest culture. Give her chances to draw inspiration from the beautiful in nature and in art. And, above all, insure her some respite from labor, and some tranquillity. Unless these conditions are observed, "but little can be done to shape and conduct the home with reference to the higher mental needs of the children who live in it."

I once heard "Grace Greenwood" tell a little story which ought to come in here, for our own object is to make out as strong a case as we possibly can. We want to prove that mothers must have culture because they are mothers. We want to show it to be absolutely necessary for woman, in the accomplishment of her acknowledged mission. When this fact is recognized, then culture will take rank with essentials, and receive attention as such.

"Grace Greenwood" said that a friend of hers, a teacher "out West," had in her school four or five children from one family. The parents were poor, ignorant, and of the kind commonly called low, coarse sort of people. The children, with one exception, were stupid, rough-mannered, and depraved. The one exception, a little girl, showed such refinement, appreciation, and quickness of apprehension, that the teacher at last asked the mother if she could account for the striking difference between this child and its brothers and sisters. The mother could not. The children had been brought up together there in that lonely place, had been treated alike, and had never been separated. She knew the little girl was very different from her brothers and sisters, but knew not the reason why. The teacher then asked, "Was there any thing in your mode of life for the months preceding her birth, that there was not in the corresponding time before the births of the others?" The mother at first answered decidedly that there was nothing; but after thinking a few moments said, "Well, there was one, a very small thing, but that couldn't have had any thing to do with the matter. One day a peddler came along; and among his books was a pretty, red-covered poetry book, and I wanted it bad. But my husband said he couldn't afford it, and the peddler went off. I couldn't get that book out of my mind;

and in the night I took some of my own money, and travelled on foot to the next town, found the peddler, bought the book, and got back before morning, and was never missed from the house. That book was the greatest comfort to me that ever was. I read it over and over, up to the day my child was born."

Also would come in well here that oft-told story of a pauper named "Margaret," who was once "set adrift in a village of the county ... and left to grow up as best she could, and from whom have descended two hundred criminals. The, whole number of this girl's descendants, through six generations, is nine hundred; and besides the 'two hundred' a large number have been idiots, imbeciles, drunkards, lunatics, and paupers."

Friends, to say nothing of higher motives, would it not be good policy to educate wisely every girl in the country? Are not mothers, as child-trainers, in absolute need of true culture? In cases where families depend on the labor of their girls, perhaps the State would make a saving even by compensating these families for the loss of such labor. Perhaps it would be cheaper, even in a pecuniary sense, for the State to do this, than to support reformatory establishments, prisons, almshouses, and insane-asylums, with their necessary retinues of officials. Institutions in which these girls were educated might be made self-supporting, and the course of instruction might include different kinds of handicraft.

It was poor economy for the State to let that pauper "grow up as best she could." It would probably have been money in the State's pocket had it surrounded "Margaret" in her early childhood with the choicest productions of art, engaged competent teachers to instruct her in the solid branches, in the accomplishments, in hygiene, in the principles and practice of integrity, and then have given her particular instruction in all matters connected with the training of children. And had she developed a remarkable taste for painting, for modelling, or for music, the State could better have afforded even sending her to Italy, than to have taken care of those "two hundred criminals," besides "a large number" of "idiots, imbeciles, drunkards, lunatics, and paupers."

CHAPTER IV.
THE OTHER PART OF "WOMAN'S MISSION."--RUFFLES VERSUS READING.--THE CULTIVATION OF THE FINGERS.

Let us leave for a while this matter of child-training, and consider the other part of woman's mission,--namely, "making home happy." It would seem that even for this the wife should be at least the equal of her husband in culture, in order that the two may be in sympathy. When a loving couple marry, they unite their interests, and it is in this union of interests that they find happiness. We often hear from a wife or a husband remarks like these: "I only half enjoyed it, because he (or she) wasn't there;" "It will be no pleasure to me unless he (or she) is there too;" "The company were charming, but still I felt lonesome there without him (or her)." The phrase "half enjoy" gives the idea; for a sympathetic couple are to such a degree one that a pleasure which comes to either singly can only be half enjoyed, and even this half-joy is lessened by the consciousness of what the other is losing. In a rather sarcastic article, taken from an English magazine, occur a few sentences which illustrate this point very well. The writer is describing a honeymoon:--

"The real difficulty is to be entertaining. The one thirst of the young bride is for amusement, and she has no idea of amusing herself. It is diverting to see the spouse of this ideal creature wend his way to the lending library, after a week of idealism, and the relief with which he carries home a novel. How often, in expectation, has he framed to himself imaginary talks,--talk brighter and wittier than that of the friends he forsakes! But conversation is difficult in the case of a refined creature who is as ignorant as a Hottentot. He begins with the new Miltonic poem, and finds she has never looked into 'Paradise Lost.' He plunges into the Reform Bill; but she knows nothing of politics, and has never read a leading article in her life. Then she tries him, in her turn, and floods him with the dead chat of the town and an ocean of family tattle. He finds himself shut up for weeks with a creature who takes an interest in nothing but Uncle Crosspatch's temper and the scandal about Lady X. Little by little the absolute pettiness, the dense dulness, of woman's life, breaks on the disenchanted devotee. His deity is without occupation, without thought, without resources. He has a faint faith in her finer sensibility, in her poetic nature: he fetches his Tennyson from his carpet-bag, and wastes 'In Memoriam' on a critic who pronounces it pretty!"

In cases of this kind, the half-joy is strikingly apparent. We see that a husband possessing culture is likely to be lonesome among his poets and his poetry, his works of reform, and his lofty ideas, unless--she is there too.

If it be said that learned women are prone to think lightly of home comforts and home duties, to despise physical labor, to look down on the ignorant, let us hasten to reply that learning is not culture, and that we want not learned mothers, but enlightened mothers, wisely educated mothers. And let us steadfastly and perseveringly assert that enlightenment and a wise education are essential to the accomplishment of the mother's mission. When the housefather feels the truth of this, then shall we see him bringing home every publication he can lay his hands on which treats intelligently of mental, moral, or physical training. Then shall we hear him saying to the house-mother, "Cease, I pray you, this ever-lasting toil. Read, study, rest. With your solemn responsibilities, it is madness thus to spend yourself, thus to waste yourself." In his home shall the true essentials assume that position which is theirs by right, and certain occupations connected with that clamorous square inch of surface in the upper part of the mouth shall receive only their due share of attention. For in one way or another, either by lessening the work or by hiring workers, the mother shall have her leisure.

And what will women, what will the house-mothers, do when they feel this truth? Certainly not as they now do. Now it is their custom to fill in every chink and crevice of leisure time with sewing. "Look," said a young mother to me: "I made all these myself, when holding the baby, or by sitting up nights." They were children's clothes, beautifully made, and literally covered with ruffles and embroidery. Oh the thousands of stitches! The ruffles ran up and down, and over and across, and three times round. Being white, the garments were of course changed daily. In the intervals of baby-tending, the mother snatched a few minutes here and a few minutes there to starch, iron, flute, or crimp a ruffle, or to finish off a dress of her own. This "finishing off" was carried on for weeks. When her baby was asleep, or was good, or had its little ruffles all fluted, and its little sister's little ruffles were all fluted, then would she seize the opportunity to stitch, to plait, to flounce, to pucker, and to braid. Wherever a hand's breadth of the original material was left visible, some bow, or band, or queer device, was fashioned and sewed on. This zealous individual, by improving every moment, by sitting up nights, by working with the baby across her lap, accomplished her task. The dress was finished, and worn with unutterable complacency. It is this last part which is the worst part. They have no misgivings, these mothers. They expect your warm approval. "I can't get a minute's time to read," said this industrious person; and, on another occasion, "I'll own up, I don't know any thing about taking care of children." Swift, speaking of women, said that they "employ more thought, memory, and application to become fools than would serve to make them wise and useful;" and perhaps he spoke truly. For suppose this young mother had been as eager to gain ideas as she was to accomplish a bias band, a French fold, or a flounce. Suppose that, in the intervals of baby-tending, instead of fluting her little girls' ruffles and embroidering their garments, she had tried to snatch some information which would help her in the bringing up of those little girls. The truth is, mothers take their leisure time for what seems to them to be first in importance. It is easy to see what they consider essentials, and what, from them, children are learning to consider essentials. The "knowingness" of some of our children on subjects connected with dress is simply appalling. A girl of eight or ten summers will take you in at a glance, from topmost plume to boot-tap, by items and collectively, analytically and synthetically. She discourses, in technical terms, of the fall of your drapery,--the propriety of your trimmings, and the effect of this, that, or the other. She has a proper appreciation of what is French in your attire, and a proper scorn of what is not. She recognizes "real lace" in a twinkle of her eye, and "all wool" with a touch of her finger-tips. Plainly clad school-children are often made to suffer keenly by the cutting remarks of other school-children sumptuously arrayed. A little girl aged six, returning from a child's party, exclaimed, "O mamma!

What do you think? Bessie had her dress trimmed with lace, and it wasn't real!"

The law, "No child shall walk the street in a plain dress," is just as practically a law as if it had been enacted by the legal authorities. Mothers obey its high behests, and dare not rebel against it. Look at our little girls going to school, each with her tucks and ruffles. Who "gets time" to do all that sewing? where do they get it, and at what sacrifices? A goodly number of stitches and moments go to the making and putting on of even one ruffle on one skirt. Think of all the stitches and moments necessary for the making and putting of all the ruffles on all the skirts of the several little girls often belonging to one family! What a prospect before her has a mother of little girls! And there is no escape, not even in common sense. A woman considered sensible in the very highest degree will dress her little girl like other little girls, or perish in the attempt. How many do thus perish, or are helped to perish, we shall never know. A frail, delicate woman said to me one day, "Oh, I do hope the fashions will change before Sissy grows up, for I don't see how it will be possible for me to make her clothes." You observe her submissive, law-abiding spirit. The possibility of evading the law never even suggests itself. There is many a feeble mother of grown and growing "Sissys" to whom the spring or fall dressmaking appears like an avalanche coming to overwhelm her, or a Juggernaut coming to roll over her. She asks not, "How shall I escape?" but, "How shall I endure?" Let her console herself. These semi-annual experiences are all "mission." All sewing is "mission;" all cooking is "mission." It matters not what she cooks, nor what she sews. "Domestic," and worthy all praise, does the community consider that woman who keeps her hands employed, and is bodily present with her children inside the house.

But her bodily presence, even with mother love and longing to do her best, is not enough. There should be added two things,--knowledge and wisdom. These, however, she does not have, because to obtain them are needed what she does not get,--leisure, tranquillity, and the various resources and appliances of culture; also because their importance is not felt even by herself; also because the community does not yet see that she has need of them. And this brings us round to the point we started from,--namely, that the present unsatisfactory state of things is owing largely to the want of insight, or ***unenlightenment***, which prevails concerning what woman needs and must have in order rightly to fulfil her mission.

CHAPTER V.
OTHER CAUSES CONSIDERED.--MASCULINE IDEA OF WOMAN'S WORK.

Another supporting cause, as we may call it, of the existing state of things is the ignorance of mankind concerning the cost of carrying on the family,--not the cost to themselves in money, but the cost to woman in endurance. Of its power to exhaust her vital forces they have not the remotest idea. Each of its little ten-minute duties seems so trifling that to call it work appears absurd. They do not reflect that often a dozen of these ten-minute duties must be crowded into an hour which holds but just six ten-minutes; that her day is crowded with these crowded hours; that consequently she can never be free from hurry, and that constant hurry is a constant strain upon her in every way. They themselves, they think, could do up the work in half the time, and not feel it a bit. Scarcely a man of them but thinks the dishes might be just rinsed off under the faucet, and stood up to dry. Scarcely a man of them who, if this were tried, would not cast more than inquiring glances at his trencher; for it is always what is not done that a man sees. If one chair-round escapes dusting, it is that chair-round which he particularly notices. In his mind then are two ideas: one is of the whole long day, the other of that infinitesimal undone duty. The remark visible on his countenance is this: "The whole day, and no time to dust a chair-round!"

> "The painful warrior famoused for fight,
>   After a thousand victories, once foiled,
>   Is from the book of honor razed quite,
>   And all the rest forgot for which *she* toiled."

Many a toiling housewife, warring against untidiness, has felt the truth of these lines, though she may not have known that the great poet embodied it in words.

One mistake of man's is, that he does not look upon the tidy state of a room as a result, but as one into which, if left to itself, it would naturally fall and remain. We know, alas! too well, that every room not only has within itself possibilities of untidiness, but that its constant tendency is in that direction, which tendency can only be checked by as constant a vigilance. Again, husbands do not always seem to understand plain English. There are certain expressions in common use among women, which, if husbands did understand plain English, would make them sadder and wiser men. "I'm completely used up;" "I never know what 'tis to feel rested;" "I'm too tired to sleep;" "I'm as tired in the morning as when I go to bed;" "Every nerve in me throbs so that I can't go to sleep;" "The life has all gone out of me;" "I am crazed with cares;" "The care is worse than the work;" "Nothing keeps that woman about the house but her ambition;" "It is the excitement of work that keeps her up." Now, how is it that a woman works on after she is completely used up? What is the substance, the capacity of this "ambition" on which alone she lives? A friend of mine, in answer to a suggestion that she should stop and take a few days' rest, said, "I don't dare to stop. If I let down, if I give way for ever so little while, I never could go on again." Think of living always in this state of tension! The dictionary definition of "tension" is "a peculiar, abnormal, constrained condition of the parts, arising from the action of antagonistic forces, in which they endeavor to return to their natural state." Exactly. There are thousands of women in just this condition, sustained there by the daily pressure and excitement of hurry, and by a stern, unyielding "must." In the treadmill of their household labor, breakfast, dinner, and supper revolve in ceaseless course, and they *must* step forward to meet them. And, when more of her vitality is expended daily than is daily renewed by food and rest, woman does, actually and without any figure of speech, use herself up. Yes, she burns herself for fuel, and goes down a wreck,--not always to death; often it is to a condition made wretched by suffering, sometimes to insanity.

I would not have believed this last had I not found it in print. In an English magazine occurs the following passage: "Some whose eyes follow these lines will recollect disagreeable seasons when their attention was distracted by conflicting cures and claims; when no one thing, however urgent, could be finished, owing to the intrusion of one or more inevitable distractions. A continued course of such inroads on the mind's serenity could be supported but by few intellects. Most pitiable is the mind's state after some hours of such distracting occupation, in which every business interferes with every other, and none is satisfactorily accomplished. Where there is a tendency to insanity it is sure to be developed by such an undesirable state of things." This is fitly supplemented by a statement made in an American magazine: "We are told that the woman's wards in the New England insane asylums are filled with middle-aged wives--mothers--driven there by overwork and anxiety."

Not long since, I heard Mr. Whittier tell the story of a woman who attempted suicide by throwing herself into the water. "Discouragement" was the reason she assigned for committing so dreadful a deed,--discouragement at the never-ending routine of household labor, and from feeling herself utterly unable to go on with it. This, with care, want of recreation, and long confinement in-doors, had probably caused temporary insanity.

The "never-endingness" of woman's work is something to be considered. A wide-awake writer, speaking of husbands and wives, says, "The out-door air, the stir, the change of ideas, the passing word for this man or that, unconsciously refresh, and lift him from the cankering care of work.... His work may be heavier, but it wears him on one side only. He has his hours sacred to business to give to his brief, his sermon, his shop. There is no drain on the rest of his faculties. She has not a power of mind, a skill of body, which her daily life does not draw upon. She asks nothing better of fate than that whatever strength she has of body and mind shall be drained for her husband and children. Now, this spirit of martyrdom is a very good thing when it is necessary. For our part, we see no occasion for it here." This is the point exactly. The "martyrdom," too often, is for objects not of the highest importance. The lack of appreciation of woman's work, as shown by man-kind in the newspapers, would be amusing, were it not saddening. Articles, dictating with solemn pomposity "what every married woman should be able to do," often appear in print, and these embodiments of (masculine) wisdom editors are eager to copy. "Every married woman should be able to cut and make her own, her husband's, and her children's clothes." The husband reads,--aloud of course, this time,--and nods approval. "To be sure, that would make a saving." The wife hears, and sighs, and perhaps blames herself that on account of her incapacity money is wasted. What the newspaper says must be true. Perhaps by sitting up later, by getting up earlier, by hurrying more, and by never setting her foot outside the door, she might follow this suggestion. "Every married woman" whose boys take to reading should snip such newspaper articles into shreds, burn them up, and bury the ashes.

Another cause of the present state of things is the lowness of the standard which has been set up for woman to attain. We have glanced at some of the things which are expected of the woman who carries on the family. What is not expected is a point of no less significance. Neither husbands nor company claim the right to expect, in that smooth, agreeable surface mentioned at the beginning, the results of mental culture. They may be gratified at finding them; but so long as the woman is amiable, thrifty, efficient, and provides three good meals every day, they feel bound not to complain. Here are the ten "Attributes of a Wife," as grouped by one of the world's famous writers: note what he allots to education: "Four to good temper, two to good sense, one to wit, one to beauty; the remaining two to be divided among other qualities, as fortune, connection, education or accomplishments, family, and so on. Divide these two parts as you please, these minor proportions must all be expressed by fractions. Not one among them is entitled to the dignity of an integer."

The prevalent belief that woman is in some degree subordinate to man, is rather taken for granted than expressly taught, as witness a certain kind of legend often told to young girls: "Once upon a time a young man, visiting a strange house, saw a damsel putting dough into pans, and saw that the dough which stuck to the platter was left sticking there; whereupon the young man said, 'This is not the wife for me.'" In another house he sees a damsel who leaves not the dough which sticks to the platter; and he says, "This is the wife for me." Another young man offers to successive maidens a skein of tangled silk to wind. The first says, "I can't;" the second tries, and gives up; the third makes a quick job of it with her scissors; the fourth spends hours in patiently, untangling, and is chosen. Now, what shows the state of public sentiment is the fact that in none of these legends is it intimated that the young man was fortunate in securing a thrifty or a patient wife. It was the thrifty or patient young woman who was fortunate in being selected by a young man,--by any young man; for the character of the youth is never stated. There is an inference, also, in the second one given, that the "hours" of a young woman can be employed to no better purpose than that of untangling a skein of silk. All this is throwing light on our problem, for so long as so much is expected of woman physically, and so little in the way of mental acquirements; so long as it is taken for granted that she is a subordinate being, that to contribute to the physical comfort and pleasure of man, and gain his approval, are the highest purposes of her existence,--it will not be considered essential that she should acquire culture. These aims are by no means unimportant ones, or unworthy ones; but are they in all cases the highest a woman should possess?

CHAPTER VI.
REASONS FOR A CHANGE.--THE EARLY TRAINING OP WOMEN.--COMMON FALLACIES.-- THE EDUCATION OF MOTHERS.

Having glanced at the present state of things, and at some of its causes, let us show reasons why it should be changed.

A sufficient reason is, because it dwarfs the intellect, ruins the health, and shortens the lives, of so many women. Another reason is, that whereas the husband may keep himself informed on matters of general interest in literature, art, science, and progress, while the wife must give her mind to domestic activities, there is danger of the two growing apart, which growing apart is destructive of that perfect sympathy so essential to the happiness of married life. A certain librarian remarked. "If a man wants a book for himself, I pick out a solid work; if for his wife, a somewhat light and trifling one." Third, because human beings have so much in common, are so closely connected, that the good of all requires the good of each, and each of all. And here is where the shortsightedness of the aristocracy of wealth and the aristocracy of sex are strikingly apparent. They fail to see that the very inferiority of what are called the inferior classes re-acts on the superior classes. We all know how it is in the human body. An injury to one small bone in the foot may cause distress which shall be felt "all over," and shall disturb the operations of the lordly brain itself. So in the body social. The wealthy and refined, into whose luxurious dwellings enters no unsightly, no uncleanly object, may say to themselves, "Never mind those poor wretches down at the other end, huddled together in their filthy tenements. They are ignorant, they don't know how to get along; but their condition doesn't concern us, so long as our houses are light, clean, and airy."

Those poor wretches, however, because they are ignorant, because they don't know how "to get along," because they live huddled together in filthy tenements, breathing foul air, starving on bad food, become a ready prey to infectious diseases. The infectious diseases spread. Men of wealth, from the refined and cleanly quarters, encounter in their business walks representatives from the degraded and disgusting quarter, and take from them the seeds of those diseases; or, on some fatal day, a miasma from the corruption of the degraded quarter is wafted in at the windows of the luxurious dwellings, and the idols of those dwellings are stricken down. So in the body politic. The wise and well-to-do enact laws, obedience to which is for the general good. The ignorant and poverty-stricken, because of their unenlightened condition, cannot see that obedience is for the good of all, and break those laws. Hence crimes, the effects of which the wise and well-to-do are made to feel, and for the punishment of which they are made to pay. It is the same with man and woman. Man says, "Let woman manage her domestic concerns, attend to her children, and gain the approbation of her husband. These are her chief duties, and for these little culture is needed." But woman becomes the mother of sons who become men; and the character, condition, and destiny of those sons who become men are, as we have seen, determined largely by the condition, pre-natal and post-natal, of the mothers. So that the ignorance in which woman is kept by man re-acts on man.

A fourth reason for a change is, that we live in a republic. In a republic every man has a voice in public affairs. Every man is first a child; and children, commonly speaking, are what the mother's influence helps to make them. Therefore, if you would have the country wisely, honestly, and decently governed, give the children the right kind of mothers. If the community knew its own interests, it would not merely permit women all possible means of culture, but would force all possible means of culture upon them. It would say, "We can't afford that you exhaust yourselves by labor, that you fritter yourselves away in vanities; for by your deficiencies we all suffer, by your losses we all lose."

But mark how stupid the community is. It desires that all its members shall possess wisdom and integrity; it declares that, in regard to character, a great deal depends on early training; it declares that this early training is the duty of mothers; and yet it does not take the next step, and say, *Therefore* mothers should be qualified for their duty, and have every facility for performing it satisfactorily. It asserts with great solemnity, "Just as the twig is bent the tree's inclined," then gives all its twigs into the hands of mothers, saying, "Here, bend these: it makes a terrible difference how they are bent, but then it is not important that you have given any attention to the process." Or, to vary the statement, the community virtually addresses woman in this way: "A fearful responsibility rests upon you. It is the responsibility of training these young, immortal souls. This is your mission, your high and holy calling. You will, however, get little time to attend to it; and, as for any special preparation or knowledge of the subject, none is required. There's a great deal of delicate and complex machinery to superintend, and a mistake will tell fearfully in the result; but, never mind, we'll trust luck." "Do we not," as Horace Mann once asked, "do we not need some single word where we can condense into one monosyllable the meaning of ten thousand fools?" Some deny the power of early training. "Look!" they say, "there is a family of children brought up just alike, and see how differently they all turn out." But a family of children should not be brought up just alike. Different temperaments require different treatment. And this is exactly the point where knowledge is necessary, and a wisdom almost superhuman. That character is the result of "inherited traits," as well as of education, does not affect the case, since children "inherit" from mothers and the sons of mothers.

CHAPTER VII.
A WAY OUT.

But suppose we leave this part of our subject, and endeavor now to find a way out of this present state of things. Let us keep the situation clearly before us. As things are, woman cannot obtain culture because of being overburdened with work and care, and also because of her enfeebled condition physically. To what is this present state of things owing? Largely to the unworthy views of both men and women concerning the essentials of life, and concerning the requirements of woman's vocation. And these unworthy views of men and women, to what are they owing? In a very great measure to early impressions. Who, chiefly, are responsible for these? Mothers. They are also, as has been shown, responsible for the larger part of the prevailing invalidism of woman. Let us be sure to bear in mind that these evils, these hinderances to culture, can be traced directly back to the influence and the ignorance of mothers; for here is where the whole thing hinges. Here is a basis to build upon. Child-training is at the beginning. Child-training is woman's work. Everybody says so. The wise say so. The foolish say so. The "oak and vine" man says so. The "private way, dangerous passing" man says so. Very good. If this is woman's work, ***educate her for her work***. If "educate" isn't the right word, instruct her, inform her, teach her, prepare her; name the process as you choose, so that it enables her to comprehend the nature of her business, and qualifies her to perform its duties. She requires not only general culture, but special preparation, a technical preparation if you will. Let this come in as the supplementary part of what is called her education. Many will pronounce this absurd; but why is it absurd? Say we have in our young woman's class at the "Institute," thirty or forty or fifty young women. Now, we know that almost every one of these, either as a mother or in some other capacity, will have the care of children. The "Institute" assumes to give these young women such knowledge as shall be useful to them in after life. If "Institutes" are not for this purpose, what are they for? One might naturally suppose, then, that the kind of knowledge which its pupils need for their special vocation would rank first in importance. And what kind will they need? Step into the house round the corner, or down the street, and ask that young mother, looking with unutterable tenderness upon the little group around her, what knowledge she would most value. She will say, "I long more than words can express to know how to keep these children well. I want to make them good children, to so train them that they will be comforts to themselves and useful to others. But I am ignorant on every point. I don't know how to keep them well, and I don't know how to control them, how to guide them."

"It is said," you reply, "that every child brings love with it. Is not love all-powerful and all-sufficient?"

"Love does come with every child; but, alas! knowledge does not come with the love. My love is so strong, and yet so blind, that it even does harm. I would almost give up a little of my love if knowledge could be got in exchange."

Here, perhaps, you inquire, somewhat sarcastically, if no instruction on these subjects was given at the "Institute." She opens wide her astonished eyes. "Oh, no! No, indeed,--surely not."

"What, then, were you taught there?"

"Well, many things,--Roman history for one. We learned all about the Punic Wars, their causes, results, and the names of the famous generals on both sides."

Now, if a Bostonian were going to Europe, it would do him no harm to be told the names of all the streets in Chicago, the names of the inhabitants of each street, with the stories of their lives, their quarrels, reconciliations, and how each one rose or fell to his position. Acquiring these facts would be good mental exercise, and from a part of them he would learn something of human nature. But what that man wants to know more than any thing is, on what day the steamer sails for Europe: is she seaworthy? what are her accommodations? is she well provisioned, well manned, well commanded? are her life-preservers stuffed with cork or shavings? So, if a man is going to build a boat, you might show him a collection of fossils, and discourse to him of the gneiss system, the mica-schist system, or talk of the atomic theory and protoplasms. Such knowledge would help to enlarge his views, extend his range of vision, and strengthen his memory, but would not help the man to build his boat. He wants to know how to lay her keel straight, how to hit the right proportions, how to make her mind her helm, how to make her go; and he has been taught that the great pachyderms are divided into paleotheria and anoplotheria. The same of our young mother: she wants to know how to bring up her child, and she has been taught "how many Punic wars there were, their causes, results, and the names of the famous generals on both sides."

It may be asked here, in what way, or by what studies, shall the young woman's class at the "Institute" be taught the necessary knowledge? It would be presumption in one like me to attempt a complete answer to that question. But the professors, presidents, and stockholders of our "Institutes" are learned and wise. If these will let their light shine in this direction as they have let it shine in other directions, a way will be revealed. But, while learning and wisdom are getting ready to do this, mere common sense may offer a few suggestions. Suppose the young woman's class were addressed somewhat in this way: "It is probable that all of you, in one capacity or another, will have the care of young children, and that for the majority it will be the chief duty of your lives. There is, then, nothing in the whole vast range of learning so important to you as knowledge on this subject." This for a general statement to begin with. As for the particular subjects and their order, common sense would ask, first, What does a young mother want to know first? First, she wants to know how to keep her child alive, how to make it strong to endure or defy disease. She needs to be taught, for instance, why a child should breathe pure air, and why it should not get its pure air in the form of draughts. She needs to know if it makes any difference what a child eats, or how often, and that a monotonous diet is injurious. She needs to know something of the nutritive qualities of different kinds of food, and why some are easy of digestion and others not, and in what way each kind builds up the system. She needs to understand the chemistry of cookery, in order to judge what kinds of food are calculated to make the best blood, bones, and muscles. She needs to have some general ideas in regard to ways of bringing back the system from an abnormal to a healthy state; as, for instance, equalizing the circulations. Learned professors, women physicians, will know how to deliver courses of lectures on all such subjects, and to tell what books have been written on them, and where these books may be found. And, as for the absurdity of teaching these things beforehand, compare that with the absurdity of rearing a race to hand over to physicians and undertakers, and choose between. And even apart from their practical bearing, why are not such items of knowledge as well worth learning, as simply items of knowledge, as the hundreds of others which, at present, no young woman's course can be without? There is no doubt that if mothers were given a knowledge of these matters beforehand, instead of being left to acquire it experimentally, the present frightful rate of infant mortality (nearly twenty-five per cent) would be reduced. Plenty of light has been thrown on this subject, but the community does not receive it. Here is some which was contributed to one of the Board of Health reports by a physician.

"The mother," he says, "requires something more than her loving instincts, her ready sympathies. With all her good-will and conscientiousness, mistakes are made. The records of infant mortality offer a melancholy illustration of the necessity of the mother's previous preparation for the care of her children. The first-born die in infancy in much larger proportion than their successors in the family. The mother learns at the cost of her first child, and is better prepared for the care of the second, and still better for the third and fourth, whose chances of development into full life and strength are much greater than those of the oldest brothers and sisters."

Think of the mother learning "at the cost of her first child," and of the absurd young woman learning beforehand; and choose between. Also please compare the "previous preparation" here recommended with the mere bureau-drawer preparation, which is the only one at present deemed necessary. Another writer, an Englishman, speaking of the high rate of infant mortality, says, "It arises from ignorance of the proper means to be employed in rearing children," which certainly is plain language. Such facts and opinions as these would make an excellent basis for a course of lectures at the "Institute," to be given by competent women physicians. The advertisements of "Mrs. Winslow's Soothing Syrup" would be remarkably suggestive in this connection. A mother of three little children said to me, "I give the baby her dose right after breakfast; and she goes to sleep, and sleeps all the forenoon. That's the way I get my work done." We all know why the baby sleeps after taking its dose. We do not know how many mothers adopt this means of getting their work done; but the fact that the proprietor of this narcotic gained his immense wealth by the sale of it enables us to form some idea.

The importance of educating nursery-girls for their calling, and the physical evils which may arise from leaving young children entirely to the care of nursery-girls, would be exceedingly suggestive as lecture subjects. Mr. Kingsley asks, "Is it too much to ask of mothers, sisters, aunts, nurses, and governesses, that they should study thrift of human health and human life by studying somewhat the laws of life and health? There are books--I may say a whole literature of books--written by scientific doctors on these matters, which are, to my mind, far more important to the schoolroom than half the trashy accomplishments, so called, which are expected to be known by our governesses."

But, supposing a mother succeeds in keeping her child alive and well, what knowledge does she desire next? She desires to know next how to guide it, influence it, mould its character. She does all these, whether she tries to or not, whether she knows it or not, whether she wishes to or not. Says Horace Mann, "It ought to be understood and felt, that in regard to children all precept and example, all kindness and harshness, all rebuke and commendation, all forms, indeed, of direct or indirect education, affect mental growth, just as dew, and sun, and shower, or untimely frost, affect vegetable growth. Their influences are integrated and made one with the soul. They enter into spiritual combination with it, never afterward to be wholly decompounded. They are like the daily food eaten by wild game, so pungent in its nature that it flavors every fibre of their flesh, and colors every bone in their bodies. Indeed, so pervading and enduring is the effect of education upon the youthful soul, that it may well be compared to a certain species of writing ink, whose color at first is scarcely perceptible, but which penetrates deeper and grows blacker by age, until, if you consume the scroll over a coal-fire, the character will still be legible in the cinders."

In regard to inherited bad traits, the question arises, if even these may not be changed for the better by skilful treatment given at a sufficiently early period. Children inheriting diseased bodies are sometimes so reared as to become healthy men and women. To do this requires watchfulness and wise management. How do we know that by watchfulness and wise management children born with inherited bad traits may not be trained to become good men and women? But the majority of mothers do not watch for such traits. It seldom occurs to them that they should thus watch. Why not bring the subject to the consideration of young women "beforehand," when, being assembled in companies, they are easy of access? It is too late when they are scattered abroad, and burdened each with her pressing family duties. "Forewarned is forearmed."

Some are of the opinion that the badness which comes by inheritance cannot be changed. This is equivalent to believing that there is no help for the evil in the world. Unworthy and vicious parents are continually transmitting objectionable traits to their children, who in turn will transmit them to theirs, and so on to the end of time. Shall we fold our hands, and resign ourselves to the prospect, while our educators go on ignoring the whole matter, and leaving those who might affect a change ignorant that it is in their power to do so?

"But," says one, "the children of those people who thought so much about education, and who started with model theories, behave no better than other people's children." This may be true, and still prove nothing. "Those people" might not have thought wisely about education. Their model theories might not have been adapted to the various temperaments often found in one family. Their children might have been exceptionally faulty by nature; unsuspected inherited traits may have developed themselves, and interfered with the workings of the model theories. The failure of "those people" shows all the more the need of preparation given "beforehand," and given by those who make the subject a special study, just as the professor of history, or mathematics, or natural philosophy, makes his department a special study.

When we consider how much is at stake, it really seems as if learned and wise professors could not employ their learning and wisdom to better purpose than in devising ways of enlightening the "young woman's class" upon any and every point which has a bearing on the intellectual and moral training of children.

CHAPTER VIII.
SUGGESTIONS FOR LECTURE TOPICS.

It is not to be supposed that enlightenment on subjects pertaining to the intellectual and moral training of children can be given to a young woman in textbook fashion, cut and dried, put up in packages, and labelled ready for use. But it will be something gained to set her thinking on these subjects, to make her feel their importance, and to inform her in what books and by what writers they have been considered. All this, and more to the same purpose, could be done by lectures and discussions, for which lectures and discussions even humble common sense need be at no loss to suggest topics. There are, for instance, the different methods of governing, of reproving, of punishing, and of securing obedience; the evils of corporal punishment, of governing by ridicule, of showing temper while punishing. Then there are questions like these: How far should love of approbation be encouraged? What prominence shall be given to externals, as personal appearance, the minutia of behavior, politeness of speech? How may perfect politeness be combined with perfect sincerity? Ways of inculcating integrity. How to teach self-reliance, without fostering self-conceit. How to encourage prudence and economy, and at the same time discourage parsimony. How to combine firmness with kindness. Implicit obedience a good basis to work on. How to enter into a child's life, and make it a happy one. How not to become a slave to a child's whims. The different amounts of indulgence and of assistance which different temperaments will bear. How shall liberality be inculcated, and extravagance denounced? On deceitfulness as taught by parents. On lying as taught by parents. On the impossibility of making one theory work in a whole family of children, or always on a single child. Shall obedience be implicit, and how early in the child's life shall it be exacted? On marriages. On the true issues of life. When shall ambition and the spirit of emulation be encouraged, and when repressed? The possibility of too much fault-finding making a child callous. If mere common sense discovers so many subjects, what number may not learning and wisdom discover when their attention shall be turned in this direction?

The "nursery-girl" topic might come up again, and be considered in its moral and intellectual aspects. Some mothers see their small children only once or twice a day, while the nurse is with them constantly. This fact might be made strikingly significant by placing it side by side with Horace Mann's words: "In regard to children, all precept and example, all kindness and harshness, all rebuke and commendation, all forms, indeed, of direct or indirect education, affect mental growth, just as dew and sun and shower, or untimely frost, affect vegetable growth. Their influences are integrated and made one with the soul. They enter into spiritual combination with it, never afterward to be wholly decompounded,"--also with a previously quoted assertion, founded on actual experiments, that "it is the medium in which a child is habitually immersed" which helps most in forming the child's character. The kind of reading which falls into the hands of the young would be found to be a lecture topic of appalling interest. Striking illustrations for such lectures could be taken from the advertisements and statistics of story-paper and dime-novel publishers. The illustrated papers which can be bought and are bought by youth are crammed to overflowing with details of vice and barbarity. They have columns headed "A Melange of Murder," "Fillicide, or a Son killing a Father," "Lust and Blood," "Fiendish Assassination," "Particulars of the Hanging of John C. Kelly," "Carving a Darky," "An Interesting Divorce Case in Boston," "A Band of Juvenile Jack Sheppards." And the pictures match the reading,--a jealous lover shooting a half-naked girl; a father murdering his family; an inquisitive youth peering into a ladies' dressing-room. If the contents of these papers are bad for us to hear of, what must they be to the youth who read them? Dime novels are advertised in these same papers as being issued once a month, and supplied by all the news companies, "Sensational stories from the pens of gifted American novelists!" "The Sharpers' League," "Lyte, or the Suspected One," "The Pirate's Isle," "Darrell, the Outlaw," "The Night Hawks, containing Midnight Robbery, Plots dark and deep," "The Female Poisoner," "Etne of the Angel Face and Demon Heart," "The Cannibal Kidnappers, a Sequel to the Boy Mutineers," "Life for Life, or the Spanish Gipsy Girl," "Tom Wildrake's Schooldays." Some of these papers are entitled "Boys' and Girls'" weeklies. The old saying is, "Build doves' nests, and doves will come." What kind of "nests" are being built by the young readers of these publications, of which it may almost literally be said, "no boy can do without one"? The boy at school has one between the leaves of his geography; the boy riding, or sailing, or resting from his work or his play, draws one from his pocket; the grocer's boy comes forward to serve you, tucking one under his jacket. In the way of statistics, it might be stated that nineteen tons of obscene publications and plates for the same were seized at one time in New-York City. Should representatives of "our best families" ask, "How does this affect us and ours?" it could be answered that catalogues of academies and boarding-schools are obtained, and that these publications are then forwarded to pupils by mail.

Topics of this kind would naturally suggest those of an opposite kind, as modes of awakening in children an appreciation of the beauty, the sublimity, the wonderfulness, of the various objects in the world of nature; also of cultivating in their minds a taste for the beautiful and the refined in art, literature, manners, conversation. These considerations could be effectively introduced into a lecture or lectures "On the Building of Doves' Nests." Is it not "essential" that mothers should have the time, the facilities, and the knowledge necessary for accomplishing what is here suggested, and that they be made sensible of its importance? But there is many a busy mother now who can scarcely "take time" to look out when her children call her to see a rainbow, much less to walk out with them among natural objects.

The object of these lectures should not be to teach any particular theories on which to act in the management of children, but to so instruct, so to enlighten young women, that when the time for action comes they will act intelligently. With the majority of women the management of children is a mere "getting along." In this "getting along" they often have recourse to deception; thus teaching deceitfulness. They are often unfair, punishing on one occasion what they smile at or wink at on another; thus teaching injustice. They lose self-control, and punish when in anger; thus setting examples of violence and bad temper. It is probable that a young woman who had been educated with a view to her vocation would be more likely to act wisely in these emergencies and in her general course of management, than one who had not. There would be more chance of her taking pains to consider. She would not work so blindly, so aimlessly, so "from hand to mouth," as do some of our mothers.

Such enlightenment is an enlightenment for which any good mother will be thankful. She wants it to work with. She feels the need of it every hour in the day. Why, then, is it not given to young women as a part of their education, and as the most important part? They are instructed in almost every thing else. They can give you the areas, population, boundaries, capitals, and peculiarities of far-away and in-significant provinces; the exact measurements of mountain ranges, lakes, and rivers; statistics, in figures, of the farthest isle beyond the farthest sea. They are lectured on the antediluvians, on the Milky Way, on the Siamese, Japanese, North Pole, on all the ologies; on the literature, modes of thought, and modes of life, of extinct races. They can converse in foreign tongues; they are familiar with dead languages, and with the superstitions, observances, and quarrels of certain races, barbarous or otherwise, who existed thousands of years ago. In fact, they are taught, after some fashion, almost every thing except what their life-work will specially require. Little will it avail a mother in her seasons of perplexity or of bereavement to remember "what wars engaged Rome after the Punic Wars, and how many years elapsed before she was mistress of the Mediterranean." This and the following questions are taken from the "Examination Papers" of a popular "Institute" for young ladies.

"Give names and dates of the principal engagements of the Persian wars, with the names of the great men of Greece during that period."

"Show cause, object, and result of the Peloponnesian war."

"Give names and attributes of the seven kings of Rome."

"After the kings were driven out, what does the internal history mainly consist of?"

"What were the social, and what were the civil wars?"

Common sense might ask why every child born in the nineteenth century must go to work so solemnly to learn the minute particulars of those old wars! Still common sense would not declare such knowledge to be altogether worthless; it would only suggest that woman wants the kind which will help her in her special department, more than she wants this kind. Said a lady in my hearing,--an only child reared in the very centre of wealth and culture,--"I was most carefully educated; but, when I came to be the mother of children, I found myself utterly helpless."

It is gratifying to know that in regard to these matters common sense has very respectable learning and wisdom on its side. A celebrated writer and thinker says, "If by some strange chance not a vestige of us descended to the remote future, save a pile of our school-books, or some college examination papers, we may imagine how puzzled an antiquary of the period would be on finding in them no indication that the learners were ever likely to be parents. 'This must have been the curriculum for their celibates,' we may fancy him concluding: 'I perceive here an elaborate preparation for many things; especially for reading the books of extinct nations (from which, indeed, it seems clear that these people had very little worth reading in their own tongue), but I find no reference whatever to the bringing up of children. They could not have been so absurd as to omit all training for this gravest of responsibilities. Evidently, then, this was the school-course of one of their monastic orders.' Seriously, is it not an astonishing fact, that though on the treatment of offspring depend their lives or their deaths, and their moral welfare or ruin, not one word on such treatment is ever given to those who will hereafter be parents? Is it not monstrous, that the fate of a new generation should be left to the chances of unreasoning custom, impulse, fancy, joined with the suggestions of ignorant nurses and the prejudiced counsel of grandmothers? To tens of thousands that are killed, add hundreds of thousands that survive with feeble constitutions, and millions that grow up with constitutions not so strong as they should be, and you will have some idea of the curse inflicted on their offspring by parents ignorant of the laws of life. With cruel carelessness they have neglected to learn any thing about these vital processes which they are unceasingly affecting by their commands and prohibitions; in utter ignorance of the simplest physiological laws, they have been, year by year, undermining the constitutions of their children, and have so inflicted disease and premature death not only on them but on their descendants. Consider the young mother and her nursery legislation. But a few years ago she was at school, where her memory was crammed with words, names, and dates; where not one idea was given her respecting the methods of dealing with the opening mind of childhood. The intervening years have been passed in practising music, in fancy work, in novel-reading, and in party-going; no thought having been yet given to the grave responsibilities of maternity. And now see her with an unfolding human character committed to her charge,--see her profoundly ignorant of the phenomena with which she has to deal, undertaking to do that which can be done but imperfectly even with the aid of the profoundest knowledge.... Lacking knowledge of mental phenomena, with their causes and consequences, her interference is frequently more mischievous than absolute passivity would have been."

This writer, it seems, would also have young men educated with a view to their probable duties as fathers, and so, of course, would we all; and much might be said on this point, especially of its bearing on the solution of our problem; still, as Mr. Frothingham said in a recent address, "The mother, of all others, is the one to foster and control the individuality of the child." It was "good mothers" which Napoleon needed in order to secure the welfare of France. "Such kind of women as are the mothers of great men," is a significant sentence I have seen somewhere in print. In fact, so much depends on mothers, that there seems no possible way by which our problem can be fully solved until the right kind of mothers shall have been raised up, and their children be grown to maturity.

CHAPTER IX.
WAYS OF IMMEDIATE ESCAPE.

But is there no possible way by which mothers now living may escape from this present unsatisfactory condition? Yes; but not many will adopt it. Simplicity in food and in dress would set free a very large number. A great part of what are called their "domestic" occupations consists in the preparation of food which is worse than unnecessary. A great part of their sewing work consists in fabricating "trimmings" which are worse than useless, even considering beauty a use, which it is. Let these simplify their cooking and their dressing, and time for culture will appear, and for them our problem be solved. We preach against the vice of intemperance, and with reason. Let us ask ourselves if intemperance in eating and in dressing is not even more to be deplored. The former brings ruin to comparatively a few: by means of the latter the whole tone of mind among women is lowered; and we have seen what it costs to lower the tone of mind among women. We must remember that not only is the condition of the mother reflected in the organism of her child, but that the child is taught by the daily example of its mother what to look upon as the essentials of life. "I feel miserable," said a feeble house-mother, just recovering from sickness; "but I managed to crawl out into the kitchen, and stir up a loaf of cake." Now, why should a sick woman have crawled out into the kitchen, to stir up a loaf of cake? Was that a paramount duty,--one which demanded the outlay of her little all of strength? This is the obvious inference, and one which children would naturally draw. A lady of intelligence, on hearing this case stated, expressed the opinion that the woman did no more than her duty. Said this lady, "If her husband liked cake, it was her duty to provide it for him at whatever sacrifice of health on her own part."

Now, it seems reasonable to suppose that an affectionate couple would have a mutual understanding in regard to such matters. It seems reasonable to suppose that an affectionate husband would rather partake of plain fare in the society of a wife with sufficient health and spirits to be companionable, than to eat his cake alone while she was recovering from the fatigue of making it.

Speaking of inferences, it is obvious what ones a child will draw from seeing its mother deprive herself of sleep and recreation and reading-time in order to trim a suit à la mode. And these inferences of children concerning essentials have a mighty bearing on our problem. Some ladies defend the present elaborate style of dress on the ground that it affords the means of subsistence to sewing-girls. There is something in this, but I think not so much as appears. Go into the upper lofts where much of this sewing is done, and what will you find? You will find them crowded with young girls, bending over sewing-machines, or over work-tables, breathing foul air, and, in some cases, engaged in conversations of the most objectionable character. Their pay is ridiculously small,--a dollar and a half for doing the machine-work on a full-trimmed fashionable "suit." I learned this, and about the conversations, from a worker at one of these establishments. Clothes, especially outside clothes, they must have and will have; consequently the saving must be made on food. Some, too poor to pay board, hire attic rooms, and pinch themselves in both fire and food. They often carry their dinner, say bread, tea, and confectioner's pie, and remain at the store all day. They are liable to be thrown among vile associates; they are exposed to many temptations. They enrich their employers, but not themselves. In dull seasons their situation is pitiable, not to say dangerous. A great number of them come from country homes. Of these, many might live comfortably in those homes, and others might earn a support by working in their neighbors' houses, where they would be considered as members of the families, have good lodging and nourishing food, and where their assistance is not only desired, but in some cases actually suffered for. They prefer the excitements of city life. (Of course, these remarks do not apply to all of them.) Fashionable ladies may not employ shop-girls directly or indirectly, but their example helps to make a market for the services of these girls. Another consideration is, that the poor seamstress who is benefited directly by the money of fashionable ladies is taught as directly, by their example, false views as to the essentials of life; so that what helps in one way hinders in another. All this should be considered by those who bring forward "sewing-girls' needs" as an argu-

ment for an elaborate style of dress. Even were this argument sound, it fails to cover
the case. A very large proportion of our women have not money enough to hire
their sewing done, and it is upon these that the wearisome burden falls. To keep up,
to vary with the varying fashion, they toil in season and out of season. Day after day
you will see them at their work-tables, their machines, their lap-boards; ripping,
stitching, turning, altering, furbishing; complaining often of sideache, of backache,
of headache, of aching all over; denying themselves outdoor air and exercise and
reading-time,--and all because they consider dressing fashionably an essential of
life. With them, what costs only time, health, and strength, costs nothing.

Think of this going on all over the country. Think of the sacrifices it involves.
In view of them, it really seems as if those who can afford to hire their sewing done
should give up elaborate trimmings just for example's sake. To be sure, this is not
striking at the foundation. To be sure, this is not the true way of bringing about a
reform. But, while waiting to get at the foundation, would it not be well to work
a little on the surface for the sake of immediate results? You would refrain from
taking a glass of wine if, by so doing, you made abstinence easier for your weaker
brother or sister. Why not consider the weakness of these toiling sisters? It is not
their fault that they do not see what are the true issues of life. They have not been
wisely educated. If the wealthy and influential would adopt a simple style of dress,
their doing so would be the means of relieving many overburdened women im-
mediately, and of helping them to solve the problem we are considering. It is not
wicked to dress simply, and no principle would be sacrificed. Neither would good
taste. Indeed, the latter is opposed to excessive ornamentation, whether in dress,
manners, speech, or writing. Long live beauty! Long live taste! Long live the "aes-
thetic side"! But simplicity does not necessarily imply plainness, nor homeliness,
nor uncouthness. There can be a simplicity of adornment. I am aware that acting
for example's sake is not a sound principle of action; but it is a question if it be not
duty in this particular case. A lady physician of large practice once said to me, "I see,
among poor girls, so much misery caused by this,"--meaning this rage for excessive
trimming,--"that I can scarcely bring myself to wear even one plain fold." If it be
asked, Should we not also relinquish costly fabrics, and the elegant appointments
of our dwellings? it may be answered, that "poor girls" commonly give up these as
being entirely out of their reach. They buy low-priced material, and call the dress

cheap which costs only their time, their strength, their sleep, and their opportunities for reading and recreation.

We all know that the right way is to so educate woman that she will be sensible in these matters. The external life is but the natural outgrowth of the internal. It is of no use cutting off follies and fripperies from the outside so long as the heart's desire for them remains. This heart's desire must have something better in its place,--something higher, nobler, worthier. This something is enlightenment; and to effect the exchange we shall have to begin at the beginning, and enlighten the mothers. Follies and fripperies, in cooking or dressing, will give way before enlightenment, just as do the skin paintings, tattooings, gaudy colors, glass beads and tinsel, and other absurdities of savage tribes; just as have done the barbaric customs and splendors of the barbaric ages. Woman is not quite out of her barbaric stage yet. At any rate, she is not fully enlightened. The desire for that redundancy of adornment which is in bad taste still remains. In the process of evolution, the nose-ring has been cast off; but rings are still hooked into the flesh of the ears, and worn with genuine barbaric complacency. When women are all wisely educated, our problem will melt away and disappear. The wisely-educated woman will, of her own accord, lay hold on essentials and let go unessentials. She will do the best thing with her time, the best thing with her means. She may conform to fashion, but will not feel obliged to do so. In fact, when women become enlightened, non-conformity to fashion will be all the fashion. Right of private judgment in the matter will be conceded. All women shall dress as seemeth to them good; and no woman shall say, or think, or look, "Why do ye so?" Those having insufficient means and time will be so wise as not to feel compelled to dress like those who have plenty of both.

Meanwhile, as an immediate measure of relief, suppose a dozen or twenty mothers in each town should agree to adopt a simple yet tasteful style of dress for themselves and their little girls. This would lighten, at once, their heavy burden of work, give them "time to read," and would be a benefit to those little girls in many ways.

Another way of immediate escape is by making the present race of husbands aware that their wives are being killed, or crazed, with hard work and care, especially husbands in the small towns and villages, and more especially farmers. In regard to these last, it is no exaggeration to say that their wives in many cases work like slaves. Indeed, this falls short of the truth, for slaves have not the added burden of responsibility. As things are now, the woman who marries a farmer often goes, as one may say, into a workhouse, sentenced to hard labor for life.

When these husbands permit their wives to "overwork," it is not from indifference, but from sheer ignorance. They don't know, they don't begin to conceive, of the labor there is in "woman's work." It is true that neither are merchant-princes aware of what it costs their wives to superintend the complicated arrangements of their establishments; to see that all the wheels, and the wheels within wheels, revolve smoothly, and that comfort and style go hand in hand; but let us consider now the farmers' wives, toiling on, and on, and on, in country towns, East, West, and all the way between. Their husbands, in not a few cases, are able to hire at least the drudgery done, and would if they only knew. A young woman from a New Hampshire village, herself an invalid from hard work, speaking to me of her mother, said, "She suffers every thing with her back. When she stoops down to the oven to attend to the pies, she has to hold on to her back, hard, to get up again." I said, "Why, I shouldn't think your father would let her make them."--"Oh," said she, "father don't understand. He's hard." One day I was sitting in the house of a young woman,--a fragile, delicate creature, scarcely able to lift the baby she was holding,--when her husband came in. He was a working man, tall and robust looking. He walked toward the pantry. "You mustn't cut a pie," the little wife called out laughing. Then turning to me, she said, with a sort of appealing, piteous glance, "He don't understand how hard it is for me to make pies." I know a young woman, not a strong woman, who, with a family of very little children, does her own work, and makes from one to two dozen pies at a common baking, "'cause hubby loves 'em." I know another, similarly situated, who gives her husband pies at breakfast as well as at other meals, because "he was brought up to them at home." Now, all these "hubbies" are loving "hubbies," but--they do not know. A friend of mine, an elderly woman lately deceased, came to her death (so her neighbors said) by hard work. "Killed with work," was the exact expression they used. She was a dear good woman; a person of natural refinement, of strict integrity, of a forgiving spirit, intelligent, sweet-tempered, gentle-mannered; everybody loved her. Her husband is a well-to-do farmer. He inherited money and lands, and has them still. His wife, who was every thing to him, whom he could not bear out of his sight, and for whom, if he had known, he would have sacrificed money and lands, is gone. But--he did not know. "Mother" never complained. "Mother" did the cooking, did the washing, scrubbed the floors. They had "company forever," the neighbors said. "Mother" received, with smiling hospitality, all who came. Help was hard to procure; still help might and would have been procured had the husband known the case to be, as it certainly was, a case of life or death. But--he did not know: so "mother" died of work and care.

You sometimes see a woman, after hurrying through her forenoon's work, sink down entirely prostrated, too tired to speak a loud word, every nerve in her body quivering. The jar of a footfall upon the floor sets her "all a-tremble." As dinnertime approaches, you see that woman stepping briskly about the house, a light in her eye, a flush on her cheek, vivacity in her motions. She is "living on excitement;" "it is ambition which keeps her up." Her husband, coming in to his dinner, takes her briskness and vivacity as matters of course, regarding her, probably, as a woman who has nothing to do but to stay in the house all day. He has no more idea of the condition of that woman than her infant has.

There are thousands of husbands, who, if they knew, would lift the burden of at least the heaviest drudgery from their wives, thus giving them longer leases of life. But, as a rule, wives keep their bad feelings to themselves. They know that "a complaining woman" is a term of reproach. They are exhorted in newspaper after newspaper to "make home happy by cheerful looks and words." They wish to do so. With a laudable desire to save money, they spend themselves, and "get along" without help. It is truly a getting-along, not a living. Sometimes, however, they are obliged to mention their feebleness, or their ailments, as reasons for neglect of duty. It is astonishing how little importance, in many cases, the husband attaches to the facts thus stated. Apparently he considers ailments either as being natural to woman, or as afflictions sent upon her by the Lord. He seems to look upon her as a sort of machine, which is liable to run down, but which may easily be wound up by a little medicine, and set going again. If the medicine does not set her going again, he brings her pastor to pray for her; if she dies, he says, "The Lord hath taken her away." All this because he does not know. When husbands are enlightened on this important point, this solemn point, they will insist on less work for women. Less work implies more leisure, and with leisure comes time for culture.

Another step towards the immediate solution of our problem is, to establish the fact that woman stands on a level with man, and is neither an appendage nor a "relict." Relict, it is true, only means that which is left; still we do not hear James Smith called the "relict" of Hannah Smith. Standing on the same level does not imply a likeness, but simply a natural equality,--equality, for instance, in matters of conscience, judgment, and opinion. It is often said, that, as a barbarous race progresses toward civilization, its women are brought nearer and nearer to an equality with its men. Thus in the barbaric stage woman is an appendage to man, existing solely for his pleasure and convenience. She is then at her lowest. As civilization progresses, she rises gradually nearer an equality with man.

When she is all the way up, when her individuality is recognized as man's is recognized, then civilization, in this respect, will have done its perfect work. Woman among us is almost all the way up, but not quite. She is still considered, and considers herself, a little bit inferior by nature. We see at once how this bears upon our question. Just so much as woman is considered inferior, just so much less importance is attached to the nature of her occupations and acquirements. It is all right enough that an inferior being should devote herself to follies, or to drudgeries, or to catering to fastidious appetites. These duties are on a level with her capacities; for these she was created, and for these culture is unneeded. When civilization shall have finished its work, so far as to bring woman up to her true position of equality with man,--equality in matters of conscience, judgment, opinion, and privileges,--then will man be able to put off from his shoulders the responsibility of deciding what is, and what is not, proper for her to do. He has carried double weight long and uncomplainingly, and should in justice to himself be relieved. Equals need not decide for equals. Woman will take up the burden he throws off, and decide for herself. We must proceed cautiously here, for there are lions in the path. Being free to choose, she may choose to take interest in such kinds of public affairs as have a bearing on her special duty. We are interested in this, remember, because whatever affects her special duty affects the solution of our problem.

Now let us ask, under our breaths, what are public affairs? The public consists of individuals. If there were no individuals there would be no public. Public affairs, then, are only individual's affairs, managed collectively, because that is the most convenient way of managing them. Their good or bad management affects the comfort of men, women, and children. Let us ask, why, simply by being christened "public affairs," should they be turned into a great, horrid bugaboo, too dangerous for women even to think of? Schools are a part of public affairs, and one would suppose it to be a part of woman's vocation to ascertain what is the influence of these schools on the children she is bringing up; to learn whether they are working with her or against her. Cases might arise concerning choice of teachers, hours of study, kinds of study, ventilation, and so forth, in which it would be her duty, as a child-trainer, to express an opinion: like the following one, for instance, which comes to us in the newspapers, as "criminal negligence in the affairs at the Mount Pleasant Schoolhouse, by which about a dozen children have died of disease, others passed through severe sickness, and not a few, including teachers, made temporary invalids, or infected with boils or scrofulous sores, caused by breathing the polluted air that has infested the building from neglected earth-closets. The Board of Health officially announced that this was the cause of the sickness, and recommended the removal of the earth-closets. The janitor of the building, it seems, is incompetent, and holds his place only because he is also a member of the School Board; which suggests the query whether men unfit for janitors are usually placed on the Nashua School Committee.... Five of the lads who died were among the brightest scholars in the public schools. The building has not yet been properly renovated."

Shall woman's sons be thus destroyed, and woman be powerless to interfere?

In urgent cases like this, it might become the duty of the mother to express her opinion by dropping a slip of paper with a name written on it into a hat or a box. It would even be possible to conceive of emergencies in which these slips of paper would so affect some vital issue,--as, for instance, the choice or removal of the janitor who will furnish the air for her children to breathe,--that the father would stay with the children while the mother went out to thus express her opinion.

Then, indeed, would the climax be reached! Then would that state of things so long foretold have come to pass: the husband takes care of the children, while the wife goes out to vote! Then would the funny artist snatch up his pencil, and the funny editor his quill. It has always been a mystery to me where the laugh came in on this joke. True, it is not his calling; but what is there so very incongruous in a father's "taking care" of his own children? Fathers love their children, and will toil night and day for them, even for the very small ones. Is there any thing ridiculous, then, in their taking them in their arms, and overlooking their childish sports? A man may take a lamb in his arms without losing an iota of his dignity, and without being caricatured in any one of our weeklies. It is quite time that these precious little human lambs ceased to be the subjects of scoffs and sneers.

But we must pass on from this part of our subject, and glance at one or two other ways of immediate escape from the present unsatisfactory state of things. See how quickly such escape might be made by a truly enlightened family. First, they hold counsel together, men and women, all desiring the same object. Question, How shall "mother" find time for culture? Say the male members, "Mother's work must be lessened,--must be: there is a necessity in the case."--"But how?"--"Well, investigate. Begin with the cooking. Let's see what we can do without." Three cheers for our side! When man begins to see what cooking he can do without, woman will begin to see her time for culture. Dinners are summoned to the bar, examined, and found guilty of too great variety and of too elaborate desserts. Sentence, less variety, and fruit for dessert instead of pies, or even pudding: exception filed here in favor of simple pudding when first course is scanty or lacking. Suppers summoned, tried, and found guilty of too great variety and too much richness; sentenced to omit pies for life, and admonished by judge not to cling too closely to work-compelling cake. The time thus rescued from the usurper, Cooking, is handed over to "mother," the true heir, to have, and to hold.

Or, suppose the question to be one of health. "'Mother' works too hard. She will wear herself out."--"She doesn't complain."--"That makes no difference. She must have help."--"Where is the money coming from to pay the help?"--"Make it; earn it; dig for it; do without something; give up something; sell something; live on bread and water. Is there any thing that will weigh in the balance against 'mother's' life? We shall feel grief when she is worn out; why not when she is wearing out? We would make sacrifices to bring her back; why not to keep her with us?" The truth is, that heretofore the wrong things have been counterbalanced. Placing simple food in one scale, and dainties in the other, of course the latter outweighs the former; but place "mother's" needs and "mother's" life in one scale, and dainties in the other, and then will the latter fly up out of sight, and never be heard from any more. Councils of this kind, we must remember, are not to become general until the requirements of "woman's mission" are generally understood, and until a great many men are made aware that a great many women are killing themselves by hard work and care, and until academic professors perceive that it is wiser to give a young woman the knowledge she will want to use than that which is given for custom's sake. But how is this general enlightenment to be effected? I don't know, unless the lecturer makes these subjects the theme of his lecture, or the poet the burden of his verse, or the minister the text of his discourse.--Not proper to be brought into the church? Why not? A great deal about heathen women is brought into the church. Are American women of less account than they? Does not the condition of our women call for missionary effort? True, American wives do not sacrifice themselves for their deceased husbands, but we have seen that they are sacrificed. There is here no sacred river into which the mother hurls her newborn babe; but it has been shown, that, because American mothers are left in ignorance, a large proportion of their children drop from their arms into the dark river of death.

Should any object that such subjects are below the dignity of the church, we might reply that the church is bound to help us for the reason that the present state of things is partly owing to her efforts. The ministers of the church in past times have labored to convince people that this life for its own sake is of little account; that we were placed here, not to develop the faculties and enjoy the pleasures which pertain to this stage of our existence, but solely to prepare for another. They have taught that we sicken and die prematurely because God wills it, not because we transgress his laws. To those suffering physically from such transgression they have said in effect, "Pray God to relieve your pain, for he sent it upon you."

CHAPTER X.
MEANS OF ESCAPE ALREADY IN OPERATION.

Three effective means by which the desired change may be accomplished are, first, that women meet regularly for the purpose of discussing such matters as especially affect them and their mission; second, that they have a paper for this same object; third, that representative women from different sections of the country come together occasionally, and compare views on these matters. Such means we already have in the "Woman's Club," the "Woman's Journal," and the "Woman's Congress."

The first of these institutions is not what the uninitiated, judging from its name, might suppose. The writer, though not a club-member, can affirm of her own knowledge, that at the weekly gatherings questions are discussed which have a direct bearing on the interests of the family and household. From these gatherings, members return to their homes strengthened, refreshed, enlightened. All teachers can testify that from teachers' conventions they go back to work with awakened interest, fresh zeal, and with newly-acquired ideas. The contact of mind with mind has invigorated them. They have all taken from each other, yet none have been losers, but all have been gainers. Every school which lost its teacher for a season gained tenfold by that teacher's absence. So it is with the club meetings. Women leave their homes to consider how the standard of those homes may be raised. I happened to be present once when the discussion was upon "The amount and kind of obedience to be exacted from children;" and I said to myself, Now, this seems the right thing exactly. How natural, how sensible, for women to meet and confer on such subjects as this, each one bringing her perplexities or her suggestions; the old giving their experience, the young profiting thereby! What better could mothers do for their children than thus to meet occasionally and hold counsel together?

Still people in general do not take this view of the case. People in general are satisfied if a mother is bodily present with her children, and do not trouble themselves as to her enlightenment.

Look at the last Woman's Congress, side by side with three other large conventions held in this country not so very long ago, and compare its purposes with theirs. The questions which occupied the members of one of the three related chiefly to articles of belief, and to those particular articles of belief in which they all believed. It was stated beforehand, that the great object to be attained was unity, and that no subjects would come up which, by calling out opposing opinions, might mar the harmony of the occasion.

Another convention occupied much of its time in deciding whether those of the denomination who sit at communion with others of the denomination who have sat at communion with a person who has not been wholly immersed, shall be fellowshipped by the denomination.

An enthusiastic member of still another convention publishes a long and glowing account of its proceedings, in which account occurs the following curious paragraph:--

"During the discussions in convention, the presentation of petitions and memorials and drafts of canons, the reports of the committees on canons, the amendments and substitutes, the transit of canons back and forth between the two houses, and finally, the conference committee, the slowly developing action of the convention was under such confusion and cloud, that it was and may yet be difficult for many, especially those at a distance, to make up their mind as to what finally took place." The object of this paragraph was to account for some wrong impressions made by the published reports.

I submit that what humanity wants to know is, how to live rightly, and that it is suffering for this knowledge. It is not suffering to know all about "altar cloths" and "eucharistic lights," and "colored chasubles" and "the use of the viretta in worship." It is not suffering to know if certain persons can partake of the Lord's Supper with other certain persons who have partaken with other certain persons. It is not suffering to know that a large number of individuals believe exactly alike, and exactly as did their ancestors. How are all these agreements and disagreements to help a poor fellow who has inherited certain proclivities, and wishes to be rid of them, and that his children may overmaster them?

Humanity does want to know, right away, how to keep itself alive and well and doing well. It wants brought up for consideration the wrongs which oppress it, the evils which defile it, the crimes which degrade it; to have their causes investigated, and their remedies suggested. This is live work; and it is such work as this which occupied the attention of the Woman's Congress. No uncertain sound there. Those "at a distance," those at the very antipodes, might "make up their mind" that its members were asking themselves, what have we, as wives and mothers, to do with these things? While other conventions are "agreeing," and "fellowshipping," and wrangling over "altar cloths," and "virettas," the Woman's Congress considers matters which have an immediate practical bearing on the welfare of human beings. While the community is working away at the surface, with its prisons, its police, its hangmen, its societies for the suppression of vice, its schools for reform, its homes for the fallen (no doubt often with good results), the Woman's Congress strikes at the foundation, and by pointing out "The Influence of Literature upon Crime," and the telling effect of "Pre-natal Influences," suggests how vice may be prevented, character right-formed, and humanity kept from falling. It inquires, "How can Woman best oppose Intemperance?" It considers those two vast underlying subjects, "The Education of Women," and "The Physical Education of our Girls;" while it by no means overlooks those unfortunates whom society sets apart, and labels "fallen women."

In regard to our problem, if any light has been thrown, if, "the word" has been guessed, I should say "the word" is "enlightenment," --enlightenment of the community as to the requirements of woman's mission, enlightenment of woman herself as a preparation for that mission. What say you, friends? Shall our women receive such enlightenment? and shall it come in to the finishing or supplementary part of their education (so called)?

True, this will cause innovations; but is it *therefore* objectionable? No one will call our present system of education a perfect one; why, then, should there not be innovations? "Why, indeed," asks a writer in "The Atlantic," "except that the training of their children is the last thing about which parents and communities will exert themselves to vigorous thought and independent action? No more striking proof of the inertia of the human mind can be found," he says, "than the fact... that for many generations the true philosophy of teaching has had its prophets and apostles, and yet that substantially we are training our children in the same old blundering way." The fault of this "old blundering way," it seems to me, is its one-sidedness. It educates only the intellect. Is this the right way? Surely the moral nature is also educable. Indeed, if the mind is trained to act energetically, so much more should the moral sense be trained to control the workings of that mind. Then, since the world, we hope, is outgrowing battles, why is it considered ***essential*** that we inform ourselves so particularly, so minutely, so statistically, concerning battles fought so long, long, long ago? Does the process hasten on the time of beating swords into plough-shares? Suppose each generation, as it comes on to the stage, does inform itself thus minutely: what, in the long-run, does humanity gain thereby?

But these considerations open up subjects too vast and too important to be even mentioned in these closing chapters. Will not you who know the inevitable influence of the mother upon her children,--will you not see to it that some portion of the time devoted to her education is spent in preparing her for her life-work? Can you think of any surer way than this by which good citizens may be raised up for our country? Wickedness abounds. It is omnipresent. Every day,--yes, twice a day,--the newspapers bring us tidings of corruption, fraud, villany, not only in low places, but in high places; in exceedingly high places. Crime is on the increase. Public officials, supported and trusted by the people, hesitate not to defraud the people. Individuals in good and regular standing socially and religiously, church-members, sabbath-school teachers, defraud their nearest friends.

Nobody can tell whom to trust. If, then, neither church, nor state, nor social position, nor any outside influence, has power to make men honest, where shall we look for such power? We must look to an inside influence. The restraining power, in order to be effective in all cases, must proceed from the character of the individual; and the character of the individual is formed to a very great degree by early training; and early training comes from--women. So here we are again down to our working ground.

Let us hope that innovations will be made. Let us hope that at no distant day it will be thought as important for a young person to be made a good member of society as to be able to cipher in the "rule of three," in "alligation medial" and "alligation alternate." A recent writer, a professor in the University of Pennsylvania, urges "the importance of incorporating into our public school systems such studies and such training as will tend to educate men for their place in the body politic." He says, "A line of teaching which concerns matters of more importance to society than all the ordinary branches of knowledge put together is allowed to have no formal provision made for it." This writer recommends the study of biographies. In Locke's system good principles were to be cared for first, intellectual activity next, and actual knowledge last of all.

Suppose the young women of thirty years ago had been thoroughly instructed in hygienic laws: would not the effects of such instruction be perceptible in our present health-rates and death-rates? Let us begin now to affect the health-rates and death-rates of thirty years hence. And it will do no harm to instruct young men also in such matters. Even while I am writing these pages, a State Board of Health report comes to me, in which it is shown by facts and figures how our death-rates are affected by ignorance,--ignorance as exhibited in the locating, building, and ventilating of dwelling-houses, drainage, situation of wells, planting of trees, choice of food and cooking of the same, as well as in the management of children. Can any subjects comprised in any school course compare in importance with these? For humanity's sake, let our young people take time enough from their geographies and Latin dictionaries to learn how to keep themselves alive! It is possible too, that, if the young women of thirty years ago had been enlightened on the subject of moral and mental training, our present crime rates might be less than they are, and dishonesty and dishonor in high places and in low places be less frequent.

Mr. Whittier tells the story of a man in a certain town, who desired the removal of an old building--an almshouse, I think--from a certain locality. As the quickest way of accomplishing this, he gave a man a dollar a day on condition that this man should do nothing else but talk from morning to night with various people on the subject of having that building moved. And it was moved. The old building we have to move is made up of prejudices, ignorance, settled opinions, and firmly-established customs, and it is therefore quite time we were beginning our work. Remember the tremendous importance of our object. An Englishman, Lord Rosebury, in a recent address, insists on a special preparation for the hereditary rulers who sit in Parliament; and, if those who are to rule mind need this, how much more do they need it who are to stamp mind, and give it its first direction! Horace Mann shall close this chapter with one of his impressive sentences. Says this truly great man, "If we fasten our eyes upon the effects which education may throw forward into immortal destinies, it is then that we are awed, amazed, overpowered, by the thought that we have been placed in a system where the soul's eternal flight may he made higher or lower by those who plume its tender wings, and direct its early course. Such is the magnitude, the transcendence, of this subject."

CHAPTER XI.
SUPPLEMENTARY.

Some persons have asked, after hearing or reading the foregoing suggestions, "Do not *men* also work too much and read too little? Is not the influence of *fathers* on their children to be considered? Should not *fathers* be educated for their vocation?" To these questions there can be but one answer. Yes! and the yes cannot be too emphatic. But the paper which formed the nucleus of these chapters was written by a woman at the request of women, to be read before a woman's club assembled to consider the question, "How shall the mother obtain culture?" The very fact that such a question had suggested itself to them, shows that women feel the need of more than their present opportunities for culture. If men feel this need, there is nothing to prevent them from assembling to discuss their unsatisfactory condition, to devise ways of improving it, to consider their responsibilities, and to inquire how they shall best qualify themselves to fulfil the duties of their vocation. The writer is under the impression that men's clubs do not meet especially with a view to such discussions.

The following paragraphs comprise the first part of a letter published in "The New York Tribune."

"These letters will speak to the hearts of thousands of women all through the country, and particularly to the women "out West," as they have already to my own. This problem has been revolved in my mind again and again, but no clew has appeared by which to solve it; and I have laid it down hopelessly, feeling that there is no alternative but to submit and carry the burden as long as strength endures, and seeing no outlook for the future but in a brief period of old age, when care and labor must come on younger shoulders.

"I want to speak only of the condition of women with whom I am best acquainted,--the wives of farmers in this part of Illinois. Many instances I have known of women who received in the East an education in some cases superior to that of their husbands, but a life of constant care and drudgery has caused them to lose, instead of gain in mental culture, while the husbands have grown away from them; and it is only in subjects of a lower nature that they have a common interest. A man, in his every-day intercourse with other men, and his business calls into all kinds of places and scenes, must be a fool not to receive new ideas, not to become more intelligent on many subjects. But what can be expected of the wife, almost always at home in the isolated farm-house, in a sparsely settled community, and if poor and struggling with debt, as many are, with no reading except, one or two newspapers? If she had a library of books, it would make but little difference, for she has no time to read them. All through the Western country there is an absolute dearth of women's "help." "A girl" can hardly be obtained for love or money. Girls in towns or cities will not go into the country, and country girls are too independent. If they have a father's house, they will not leave it for any length of time, as actual want is not known here in the country. Within a radius of five miles in every direction from my home, where I have lived eight years, I have never known or heard of a family or person suffering for any thing to eat, drink, or wear; and have never had a call for help in that direction. A house-mother of my acquaintance, whose husband owns a "section" farm, suffers much from illness, and has a large family, yet for months has been without any help in her work but that of her little girls,--the oldest not over twelve,--simply because she could not get a servant. The farmers themselves are under less necessity to labor than in many other parts of the country. Farms are comparatively large, and produce large crops, and it pays them to hire laborers. Many farmers work in the field very little, while the wife and mother does the housework not only for her own family, but for from one to three laborers. During the rush of crop raising and harvesting, from April to August, she must be up at four in the morning, and she cannot have her supper until the farm work is all done; and by the time her children are put to bed, the milk cared for, and dishes washed, it is nine o'clock or after. It is hard for a woman who is hungry for reading to see how much leisure even "hired men" have to read,--their winter and rainy days, their long noonings and evenings, and odd bits of time, while she has comparatively none."

It seems, then, that it is with women as with men: at the West too few workers for the work, at the East too little work for the workers. Now, in the case of the
men, there is a regularly organized plan to bring the workers to the work. Laborers
are taken from the East where they stand in each other's way, and carried to the
West where their services are needed. Why not have some arrangement of this
kind for the women? In the present condition of things, destitute women and girls
congregate in our cities, and in dull seasons depend on charity for their daily food.
In Boston, during the last winter, this charitable feeding was reduced to a system,
and, according to published reports, immense numbers were thus supplied with
food. It seems a pity that women and girls should starve or live on charity in our
cities, while so many families in the West are suffering for their help. Can there
not be some concerted plan between these widely separated sections of the country
whereby at least a portion of our destitute ones can be conveyed to the West, and
there provided with comfortable homes?

By private letters received from "Tribune" readers living in different parts of
the country, it appears that many thoughtful people are considering our problem,
and devising ways of solving it. One of these letters says, "You sprinkle rose water
where you should pour aquafortis. You say husbands '***don't know***' that their wives
are overworked. The truth is, they don't care." The writer recommends that the
laws be so altered as to make second marriages illegal, assuming that, if a man could
have only one wife, he would take good care of that one. This is an unpleasant view
of the case, and would not be presented here, only that, from the earnest down-
rightness of the letter, it seems probable that its writer speaks from knowledge, and
represents a class,--a small one, let us hope.

Three private letters, coming one from the South, one from the East, and one
from the West, declare that woman's present state of invalidism and thraldom to
labor is occasioned by the too frequent recurrence of the duties and exhaustive demands of maternity. The writers of the letters affirm, that, in these matters, women
are often made the slaves of sensual husbands, and earnestly entreat that this shall
be mentioned among the "causes of the present state of things."

The only sure and lasting remedy for the above-mentioned evils, and others
similar to them, is a wise education. When man is wisely educated, and not till
then, will he have a proper consideration for woman.

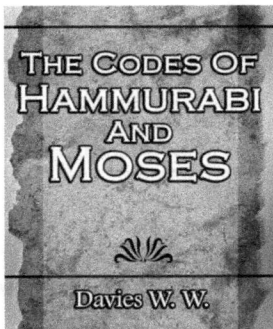

The Codes Of Hammurabi And Moses
W. W. Davies

QTY

The discovery of the Hammurabi Code is one of the greatest achievements of archaeology, and is of paramount interest, not only to the student of the Bible, but also to all those interested in ancient history...

Religion   ISBN: *1-59462-338-4*   Pages:132
MSRP $12.95

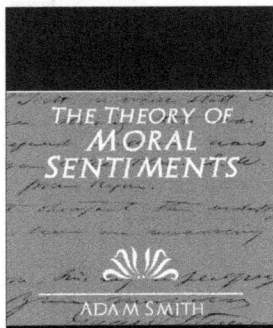

The Theory of Moral Sentiments
Adam Smith

QTY

This work from 1749. contains original theories of conscience amd moral judgment and it is the foundation for systemof morals.

Philosophy ISBN: *1-59462-777-0*   Pages:536
MSRP $19.95

Jessica's First Prayer
Hesba Stretton

QTY

In a screened and secluded corner of one of the many railway-bridges which span the streets of London there could be seen a few years ago, from five o'clock every morning until half past eight, a tidily set-out coffee-stall, consisting of a trestle and board, upon which stood two large tin cans, with a small fire of charcoal burning under each so as to keep the coffee boiling during the early hours of the morning when the work-people were thronging into the city on their way to their daily toil...

Childrens   ISBN: *1-59462-373-2*   Pages:84
MSRP $9.95

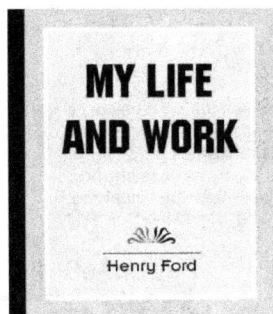

My Life and Work
Henry Ford

QTY

Henry Ford revolutionized the world with his implementation of mass production for the Model T automobile. Gain valuable business insight into his life and work with his own auto-biography... "We have only started on our development of our country we have not as yet, with all our talk of wonderful progress, done more than scratch the surface. The progress has been wonderful enough but..."

Biographies/   ISBN: *1-59462-198-5*   Pages:300
MSRP $21.95

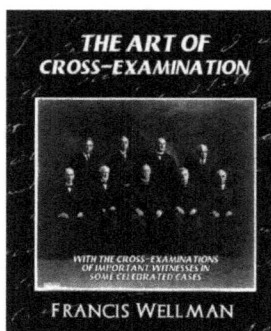

The Art of Cross-Examination
Francis Wellman

QTY

I presume it is the experience of every author, after his first book is published upon an important subject, to be almost overwhelmed with a wealth of ideas and illustrations which could readily have been included in his book, and which to his own mind, at least, seem to make a second edition inevitable. Such certainly was the case with me; and when the first edition had reached its sixth impression in five months, I rejoiced to learn that it seemed to my publishers that the book had met with a sufficiently favorable reception to justify a second and considerably enlarged edition. ..

Pages:412

Reference   ISBN: *1-59462-647-2*   *MSRP $19.95*

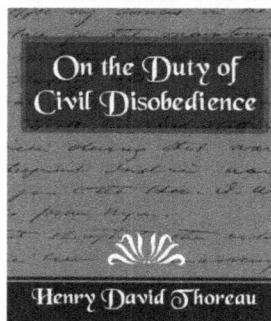

On the Duty of Civil Disobedience
Henry David Thoreau

QTY

Thoreau wrote his famous essay, On the Duty of Civil Disobedience, as a protest against an unjust but popular war and the immoral but popular institution of slave-owning. He did more than write—he declined to pay his taxes, and was hauled off to gaol in consequence. Who can say how much this refusal of his hastened the end of the war and of slavery ?

Law   ISBN: *1-59462-747-9*   **Pages:48**

MSRP $7.45

Dream Psychology Psychoanalysis for Beginners
Sigmund Freud

QTY

Sigmund Freud, born Sigismund Schlomo Freud (May 6, 1856 - September 23, 1939), was a Jewish-Austrian neurologist and psychiatrist who co-founded the psychoanalytic school of psychology. Freud is best known for his theories of the unconscious mind, especially involving the mechanism of repression; his redefinition of sexual desire as mobile and directed towards a wide variety of objects; and his therapeutic techniques, especially his understanding of transference in the therapeutic relationship and the presumed value of dreams as sources of insight into unconscious desires.

Pages:196

Psychology   ISBN: *1-59462-905-6*   *MSRP $15.45*

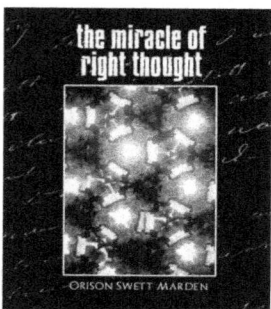

The Miracle of Right Thought
Orison Swett Marden

QTY

Believe with all of your heart that you will do what you were made to do. When the mind has once formed the habit of holding cheerful, happy, prosperous pictures, it will not be easy to form the opposite habit. It does not matter how improbable or how far away this realization may see, or how dark the prospects may be, if we visualize them as best we can, as vividly as possible, hold tenaciously to them and vigorously struggle to attain them, they will gradually become actualized, realized in the life. But a desire, a longing without endeavor, a yearning abandoned or held indifferently will vanish without realization.

Pages:360

Self Help   ISBN: *1-59462-644-8*   *MSRP $25.45*

QTY

☐ **The Rosicrucian Cosmo-Conception Mystic Christianity** *by Max Heindel*   ISBN: *1-59462-188-8*   **$38.95**
The Rosicrucian Cosmo-conception is not dogmatic, neither does it appeal to any other authority than the reason of the student. It is: not controversial, but is: sent forth in the, hope that it may help to clear...   New Age/Religion Pages 646

☐ **Abandonment To Divine Providence** *by Jean-Pierre de Caussade*   ISBN: *1-59462-228-0*   **$25.95**
"The Rev. Jean Pierre de Caussade was one of the most remarkable spiritual writers of the Society of Jesus in France in the 18th Century. His death took place at Toulouse in 1751. His works have gone through many editions and have been republished...   Inspirational/Religion Pages 400

☐ **Mental Chemistry** *by Charles Haanel*   ISBN: *1-59462-192-6*   **$23.95**
Mental Chemistry allows the change of material conditions by combining and appropriately utilizing the power of the mind. Much like applied chemistry creates something new and unique out of careful combinations of chemicals the mastery of mental chemistry...   New Age Pages 354

☐ **The Letters of Robert Browning and Elizabeth Barret Barrett 1845-1846 vol II**   ISBN: *1-59462-193-4*   **$35.95**
by Robert Browning and Elizabeth Barrett   Biographies Pages 596

☐ **Gleanings In Genesis (volume I)** *by Arthur W. Pink*   ISBN: *1-59462-130-6*   **$27.45**
Appropriately has Genesis been termed "the seed plot of the Bible" for in it we have, in germ form, almost all of the great doctrines which are afterwards fully developed in the books of Scripture which follow...   Religion/Inspirational Pages 420

☐ **The Master Key** *by L. W. de Laurence*   ISBN: *1-59462-001-6*   **$30.95**
In no branch of human knowledge has there been a more lively increase of the spirit of research during the past few years than in the study of Psychology, Concentration and Mental Discipline. The requests for authentic lessons in Thought Control, Mental Discipline and...   New Age/Business Pages 422

☐ **The Lesser Key Of Solomon Goetia** *by L. W. de Laurence*   ISBN: *1-59462-092-X*   **$9.95**
This translation of the first book of the "Lernegion" which is now for the first time made accessible to students of Talismanic Magic was done, after careful collation and edition, from numerous Ancient Manuscripts in Hebrew, Latin, and French...   New Age/Occult Pages 92

☐ **Rubaiyat Of Omar Khayyam** *by Edward Fitzgerald*   ISBN:*1-59462-332-5*   **$13.95**
Edward Fitzgerald, whom the world has already learned, in spite of his own efforts to remain within the shadow of anonymity, to look upon as one of the rarest poets of the century, was born at Bredfield, in Suffolk, on the 31st of March, 1809. He was the third son of John Purcell...   Music Pages 172

☐ **Ancient Law** *by Henry Maine*   ISBN: *1-59462-128-4*   **$29.95**
The chief object of the following pages is to indicate some of the earliest ideas of mankind, as they are reflected in Ancient Law, and to point out the relation of those ideas to modern thought.   Religion/History Pages 452

☐ **Far-Away Stories** *by William J. Locke*   ISBN: *1-59462-129-2*   **$19.45**
"Good wine needs no bush, but a collection of mixed vintages does. And this book is just such a collection. Some of the stories I do not want to remain buried for ever in the museum files of dead magazine-numbers an author's not unpardonable vanity..."   Fiction Pages 272

☐ **Life of David Crockett** *by David Crockett*   ISBN: *1-59462-250-7*   **$27.45**
"Colonel David Crockett was one of the most remarkable men of the times in which he lived. Born in humble life, but gifted with a strong will, an indomitable courage, and unremitting perseverance...   Biographies/New Age Pages 424

☐ **Lip-Reading** *by Edward Nitchie*   ISBN: *1-59462-206-X*   **$25.95**
Edward B. Nitchie, founder of the New York School for the Hard of Hearing, now the Nitchie School of Lip-Reading, Inc, wrote "LIP-READING Principles and Practice". The development and perfecting of this meritorious work on lip-reading was an undertaking...   How-to Pages 400

☐ **A Handbook of Suggestive Therapeutics, Applied Hypnotism, Psychic Science**   ISBN: *1-59462-214-0*   **$24.95**
by Henry Munro   Health/New Age/Health/Self-help Pages 376

☐ **A Doll's House: and Two Other Plays** *by Henrik Ibsen*   ISBN: *1-59462-112-8*   **$19.95**
Henrik Ibsen created this classic when in revolutionary 1848 Rome. Introducing some striking concepts in playwriting for the realist genre, this play has been studied the world over.   Fiction/Classics/Plays 308

☐ **The Light of Asia** *by sir Edwin Arnold*   ISBN: *1-59462-204-3*   **$13.95**
In this poetic masterpiece, Edwin Arnold describes the life and teachings of Buddha. The man who was to become known as Buddha to the world was born as Prince Gautama of India but he rejected the worldly riches and abandoned the reigns of power when...   Religion/History/Biographies Pages 170

☐ **The Complete Works of Guy de Maupassant** *by Guy de Maupassant*   ISBN: *1-59462-157-8*   **$16.95**
"For days and days, nights and nights, I had dreamed of that first kiss which was to consecrate our engagement, and I knew not on what spot I should put my lips..."   Fiction/Classics Pages 240

☐ **The Art of Cross-Examination** *by Francis L. Wellman*   ISBN: *1-59462-309-0*   **$26.95**
Written by a renowned trial lawyer, Wellman imparts his experience and uses case studies to explain how to use psychology to extract desired information through questioning.   How-to/Science/Reference Pages 408

☐ **Answered or Unanswered?** *by Louisa Vaughan*   ISBN: *1-59462-248-5*   **$10.95**
Miracles of Faith in China   Religion Pages 112

☐ **The Edinburgh Lectures on Mental Science (1909)** *by Thomas*   ISBN: *1-59462-008-3*   **$11.95**
This book contains the substance of a course of lectures recently given by the writer in the Queen Street Hail, Edinburgh. Its purpose is to indicate the Natural Principles governing the relation between Mental Action and Material Conditions...   New Age/Psychology Pages 148

☐ **Ayesha** *by H. Rider Haggard*   ISBN: *1-59462-301-5*   **$24.95**
Verily and indeed it is the unexpected that happens! Probably if there was one person upon the earth from whom the Editor of this, and of a certain previous history, did not expect to hear again...   Classics Pages 380

☐ **Ayala's Angel** *by Anthony Trollope*   ISBN: *1-59462-352-X*   **$29.95**
The two girls were both pretty, but Lucy who was twenty-one who supposed to be simple and comparatively unattractive, whereas Ayala was credited, as her Bombwhat romantic name might show, with poetic charm and a taste for romance. Ayala when her father died was nineteen...   Fiction Pages 484

☐ **The American Commonwealth** *by James Bryce*   ISBN: *1-59462-286-8*   **$34.45**
An interpretation of American democratic political theory. It examines political mechanics and society from the perspective of Scotsman James Bryce   Politics Pages 572

☐ **Stories of the Pilgrims** *by Margaret P. Pumphrey*   ISBN: *1-59462-116-0*   **$17.95**
This book explores pilgrims religious oppression in England as well as their escape to Holland and eventual crossing to America on the Mayflower, and their early days in New England...   History Pages 268

QTY

The Fasting Cure *by Sinclair Upton*   ISBN: *1-59462-222-1* **$13.95**
In the Cosmopolitan Magazine for May, 1910, and in the Contemporary Review (London) for April, 1910, I published an article dealing with my experiences in fasting. I have written a great many magazine articles, but never one which attracted so much attention... New Age/Self Help/Health Pages 164

Hebrew Astrology *by Sepharial*   ISBN: *1-59462-308-2* **$13.45**
In these days of advanced thinking it is a matter of common observation that we have left many of the old landmarks behind and that we are now pressing forward to greater heights and to a wider door horizon than that which represented the mind-content of our progenitors... Astrology Pages 144

Thought Vibration or The Law of Attraction in the Thought World   ISBN: *1-59462-127-6* **$12.95**
by William Walker Atkinson   *Psychology/Religion Pages 144*

Optimism *by Helen Keller*   ISBN: *1-59462-108-X* **$15.95**
Helen Keller was blind, deaf, and mute since 19 months old, yet famously learned how to overcome these handicaps, communicate with the world, and spread her lectures promoting optimism. An inspiring read for everyone... Biographies/Inspirational Pages 84

Sara Crewe *by Frances Burnett*   ISBN: *1-59462-360-0* **$9.45**
In the first place, Miss Minchin lived in London. Her home was a large, dull, tall one, in a large, dull square, where all the houses were alike, and all the sparrows were alike, and where all the door-knockers made the same heavy sound... Childrens/Classic Pages 88

The Autobiography of Benjamin Franklin *by Benjamin Franklin*   ISBN: *1-59462-135-7* **$24.95**
The Autobiography of Benjamin Franklin has probably been more extensively read than any other American historical work, and no other book of its kind has had such ups and downs of fortune. Franklin lived for many years in England, where he was agent... Biographies/History Pages 332

Name	
Email	
Telephone	
Address	
City, State ZIP	

☐ **Credit Card**   ☐ **Check / Money Order**

Credit Card Number	
Expiration Date	
Signature	

Please Mail to: Book Jungle
PO Box 2226
Champaign, IL 61825
or Fax to: 630-214-0564

ORDERING INFORMATION

web: *www.bookjungle.com*
email: *sales@bookjungle.com*
fax: *630-214-0564*
mail: *Book Jungle PO Box 2226 Champaign, IL 61825*
or PayPal *to sales@bookjungle.com*

Please contact us for bulk discounts

DIRECT-ORDER TERMS

**20% Discount if You Order
Two or More Books**
Free Domestic Shipping!
Accepted: Master Card, Visa,
Discover, American Express

www.ingramcontent.com/pod-product-compliance
Lightning Source LLC
Chambersburg PA
CBHW080055280326
41934CB00014B/3322